Curricu

and

Assessment

SOME POLICY ISSUES

This reader is one part of an Open University integrated teaching system and the selection is therefore related to other material available to students. It is designed to evoke the critical understanding of students. Opinions expressed in it are not necessarily those of the course team or of the University.

Curriculum
and
Assessment
SOME POLICY ISSUES

A Reader edited by

PETER RAGGATT

and

GABY WEINER

at the Open University

PERGAMON PRESS

OXFORD · NEW YORK · TORONTO · SYDNEY · FRANKFURT

in association with
THE OPEN UNIVERSITY

U.K.	Pergamon Press Ltd., Headington Hill Hall, Oxford OX3 0BW, England
U.S.A.	Pergamon Press Inc., Maxwell House, Fairview Park, Elmsford, New York 10523, U.S.A.
CANADA	Pergamon Press Canada Ltd., Suite 104, 150 Consumers Road, Willowdale, Ontario M2J 1P9, Canada
AUSTRALIA	Pergamon Press (Aust.) Pty. Ltd., P.O. Box 544, Potts Point, N.S.W. 2011, Australia
FEDERAL REPUBLIC OF GERMANY	Pergamon Press Gmbh, Hammerweg 6, D-6242 Kronberg-Taunus, Federal Republic of Germany

Selection and editorial material
copyright © 1985 The Open University

First edition 1985

Library of Congress Cataloging in Publication Data
Main entry under title:
Curriculum and assessment.
"This reader consists of a collection of articles which form part of the Open University Course E333, Policy-making in education"—Perf.
1. Education, Secondary—Great Britain—Curricula—Addresses, essays, lectures.   2. High schools—Great Britain—Examination—Addresses, essays, lectures.
3. Education and state—Great Britain—Addresses, essays, lectures.   I. Raggatt, Peter C. M.   II. Weiner, Gaby. III. Open University.
LB1629.5.G7C875   1985   373.19'0941   85-9371

British Library Cataloguing in Publication Data
Curriculum and assessment: some policy issues: a reader.
1. Education—Great Britain—Curricula
I. Raggatt, Peter   II. Weiner, Gaby   III. Open University
375'.00941   LB1564.G7

ISBN 0-08-032677-3 (Hardcover)
ISBN 0-08-032676-5 (Flexicover)

Printed in Great Britain by A. Wheaton & Co, Ltd., Exeter

Preface

This reader consists of a collection of articles which form part of the Open University Course E333, *Policy-making in Education*. The course critically examines ways of analysing education policy, discusses the structure and process of educational policy-making in central and local government, and analyses educational policy in practice through case studies of particular policy issues.

The primary concern of this reader is the exploration of recent changes in curriculum and assessment policy. It examines the trend towards centralized control but also offers an assessment of continuing local authority influences. Because the reader forms only one part of the course (much of which consists of written texts or broadcasts discussing issues raised in the Reader articles), it cannot claim to offer a complete picture of curriculum and assessment policy-making. The selection of articles has been made with the overall course content in mind. It has been designed to highlight specific problems, and to develop the students' critical understanding. Opinions expressed within articles are, therefore, not necessarily those of the course team nor of the university. However, the editors believe that the selection, though not comprehensive, will be useful to anyone with an interest in curriculum and assessment policy.

There are three other readers, also published by Pergamon Press, and related to case studies of educational policy which we discussed in course material. These readers are:

Policy-making in Education: the breakdown of consensus. Edited by J. Ozga and I. McNay.
Race and Gender: equal opportunity policies in education. Edited by M. Arnot.
Education, Training and Employment: towards a new vocationalism? Edited by R. Dale.

It is not necessary to become an undergraduate of the Open University in order to study the course of which this reader is part. Further information about the course associated with this book may be obtained by writing to: The Admissions Office, The Open University, PO Box 48, Walton Hall, Milton Keynes MK7 6AB.

Contents

Introduction — It's No Secret Any More:

curriculum policy in public view

PETER RAGGATT

The articles in this reader explore curriculum and assessment policy at national and local levels. They examine the intentions of participants, their actions and their responses to external influences. A number focus on the Department of Education and Science (DES). This is to be expected, as much of the activity in curriculum and assessment policy has been initiated by the DES and is inspired by the department's concern to exercise more control over the curriculum. One way in which this is being done is by using assessment as a mechanism for control, and the consequences of this on assessment policy are given particular attention. This reader is then concerned with policy changes and shifts in the balance of power, and a brief historical account of the contextual factors that led to changes in curriculum and assessment policy is therefore necessary. It is to that that we now turn.

For nearly thirty years educational policy was a product of a political consensus. The consensus had an essentially moral base forged during wartime Britain when the injustices and anomalies of prewar society had been revealed. A core assumption was that the state had a responsibility to intervene to promote the well-being of the individual; its institutional expression was the welfare state. The forerunner for the enabling legislation that established the welfare state was the 1944 Education Act. That this should be regarded as one element in a broad commitment to social reconstruction is evident from R. A. Butler's recollections of the origins of the Act:

> The challenge of the times provided a stimulus for rethinking the purposes of society and planning the reconstruction of the social system of which education formed an integral part. ... Educational problems were thus seen as an essential part of the social problem and the urgent need for educational reform was increasingly realised (Butler, 1971, p. 3).

The growth of the welfare state was necessarily accompanied by an expansion of a professional service sector. It was this group, together with administrators, who were largely responsible for delivering the goods. In these circumstances the metaphor of 'partnership' used to describe the relationships between the DES, local education authorities (LEAs) and teacher unions has much force. Discussing this notion of partnership, Maclure (1984) depicts it as a 'consensus of action, not of ideology' and of administrators in central and local government and professionals in which any two of the partners could block the third. The ability of the LEAs, represented by William Alexander as Secretary of the Association of Education Committees, and the National Union of Teachers, represented by Ronald Gould, to block initiatives from the Minister/DES was amply demonstrated by their boycott of the Curriculum Study Group established by the DES in 1962. Also notable in this respect as a statement of 'partnership', the influence of administrators and professionals within it and the lack of political activity in educational policy, was Boyle's comment: 'The biggest number (of policies) originated from what are broadly called the "educational world", if you like from the logic of the educational service itself' (Kogan, 1971, p. 89).

One product of this partnership was that curriculum policy became a largely professional matter. The Elementary and Secondary Codes had been withdrawn before the war and the 1944 Act delegated responsibility for the curriculum to LEAs and governing bodies. In the absence of any tradition of lay participation in, or control of, education the practical result was that the curriculum became the responsibility of teachers.

Teachers were not, of course, entirely free. They had a licensed or limited autonomy, constrained at the secondary level by the public examination system in the hands of university examination boards which defined worthwhile knowledge and screened entry to higher education and the professions, and at the primary level by public (mainly parental) opinion. With grammar schools as the main route to white-collar professional jobs, aspiring parents' anxieties focused on getting their children through the 11+. Provided the staff of the primary schools respected these anxieties and ambitions by emphasizing the skills tested by the 11+, which they very largely did, teachers appeared to enjoy considerable autonomy. They always worked, however, within the margin of tolerance conceded by public opinion.

Teachers and other professional groups benefited during this period from the belief in planning and expertise which supported the growth of the welfare state and the public service sector. The heart of teachers' claims to expertise lay in curriculum and teaching methods. With a favourable postwar climate, and with politicians and planners concerned with improving access to education, teachers were able to extend their claims for professional autonomy over curriculum and methods. The heyday for experts was probably the 1960s, when beliefs in the power of technology to improve social conditions was allied to existing beliefs in expertise and backed by substantial funding. It was during this period that the first public examination controlled by teachers was established (Certificate of Secondary Education) and the Schools Council was formed. The council was dominated by teacher unions, but even more indicative of professional autonomy was a constitution which asserted the principle of teacher control at the level of the individual school. The council could only offer 'advice' on request; no teacher need take any notice of its work nor, at this stage, was it structurally related to teacher centres or to teacher education.

In this context curriculum matters were professional matters. Little attention was paid to external realities—demographic changes, finance and other resources, relationships between education and other social services —except as background features, yet these, as Shipman (1981) has argued, were the focus of decision-making for politicians and administrators in central and local government. Attention instead focused on within-education matters, on Schools Council projects and then on school-based curriculum innovation. Curriculum policy was, it seemed, politically unproblematic and unconsidered. It was an area of particular neglect in the more general field of educational policy—which did not draw much research attention either.

In the past ten years or so these features have emerged as major influences on the curriculum at national and local levels. They will not be reviewed in detail in this reader because they have already been documented elsewhere in this series. They do, however, need to be noted in this introduction because they establish the climate for change and the parameters within which policy was framed.

First there was the marked change in the ideological temper at the end of the 1960s. Benchmarks in education include the resistance of a number of local authorities to the reorganization of secondary schools along comprehensive lines; publication of the Black Papers; the Great Debate; and the rise and rise of the Manpower Services Commission as a major provider of 14+ education and training. The effect of the 'request' that local authorities submit plans for comprehensive organization (Circular 10/65) should not be underestimated. It produced the first clear break in the broad consensus that had held since the war. The issue polarized along party lines. It marked the return of sectional interests and hence of adversarial politics. It strained centre–periphery relationships and by bringing education back into the political arena it undermined the working 'partnership'.

The series of Black Papers, the first of which was published in 1969, opened a new front by directly challenging the teachers' freedoms in curriculum and teaching methods. The Black Papers asserted that standards were falling and associated this with a spread of progressive (permissive) teaching methods and with comprehensive education. The appeal was to the emotions and struck responsive chords in many parents, though, as later research was to reveal, progressive methods never were widespread.

The Great Debate moved the discussion to a new level. Coats were trailed well before the debate was formally opened in October 1976. In 1974 Sir

William Pile, then Permanent Secretary in the DES, giving evidence to an OECD review group, 'did wonder aloud whether the Government could continue to debar itself from what had been termed the secret garden of the curriculum' (OECD, 1975, p. 59). This view was repeated by his successor in June 1976 who questioned 'Whether the so-called "secret garden" of the curriculum ... could be allowed to remain so secret after all, and whether the key to the door should not be found and turned' (*Education*, 1976, p. 9).

That the curriculum was by now a public matter was again shown at the DES Conference on the secondary curriculum and the needs of society at Oxford in September 1976. Representatives from the Confederation of British Industry (CBI) and the Trades Union Congress (TUC) were invited to join educationists, local authority advisers and administrators in discussions on the need for a common curriculum, the possibility of achieving consensus on the skills, values and attitudes which a common curriculum might develop, the relationship between schools and the adult world and the potential contribution of various groups in society towards the formation of policies on the secondary curriculum (HMI, 1981). The address by Sir John Methven, Director General of the CBI, outlined 'growing dissatisfaction with standards of achievement in the basic skills reached by many school leavers' and called for greater consideration of the needs of industry (*TES*, 1976, p. 2).

Subsequent publications from the DES stressed the contribution that schools could make to Britain's industrial regeneration and promoted schooling as preparation for working life. Advancing an economic ideology of education, in sharp contrast to the child-centred progressive ideology that teachers were supposed to hold, provided the DES with important allies in its drive to obtain control over the curriculum. It also enabled the department to publicly assert that its concerns in this area were equal to those of the MSC which was rapidly emerging as an aggressive competitor for control over substantial sections of educational policy and finance. The MSC was a product of the 1973 reform of the Industrial Training Boards and had developed rapidly. By the late 1970s it was the major government response to the high level of youth unemployment and its importance and power has further increased in the 1980s. One of MSC's attractions to government is its ability to disburse funds for specific activities, something which the DES is largely unable to do. The MSC promotes and funds skill-based programmes within an economic ideology. The combined effects of MSC and DES activities have been to establish a new vocationalism in education, a belief in education for its practicality and utility.

Doubts about the effectiveness of the education system had been gathering from at least the early 1970s. By 1973, when the first oil crisis hit Western economies, education was already suffering from a crisis of confidence. In part this was of the education business's own making. During the 1960s education's ability to improve the social condition had been oversold, not least by organized interests in education. By the early 1970s any gains seemed trivial against the investments made. More particularly, the evidence was accumulating that significant numbers of the school population continued to perform poorly. Some groups, of course, have never been well served by the education system. When there has been a plentiful supply of unskilled jobs this has scarcely mattered because school-leavers have been absorbed into the manufacturing and service sectors, trade services and construction work. In the new circumstances of economic recession and structural changes, both in the movement of many manufacturing jobs to the less developed countries where labour is cheap, and in the automation of many work processes, the visibly growing numbers of young unemployed contributed to the crisis of confidence in schooling. The paradox was that industry and commerce were failing to produce the jobs, but it was schools that got the blame. One obvious consequence of the loss in confidence in education was that the education service, a major consumer of public funds, was ill-equipped to defend itself as cuts in public expenditure followed the oil-fired recession.

Local government reorganization in 1974 was an added factor. Political polarization around education was one component; corporate management was another. The former ensured that education remained on political agendas, the latter that education would have to compete with other services. Educational policy was no longer the almost exclusive domain of education committees and the chief officer but, in so far as policy held resource implications, it was an agenda item for policy and resource committees, a procedure that was increasingly the norm as central government demanded cuts in public expenditure or imposed cash limits and otherwise constrained local freedoms. Power moved to the centre within local authorities, but also moved from local authorities to central government. The Treasury fixed resource parameters, the DES and the MSC set out policy priorities.

The past ten years or so have witnessed the politicization of educational policy. What should be taught in schools and how it should be assessed have become the sites of political conflict. The conceptual framework of the 1960s and early 1970s is clearly inadequate for curriculum analysis in the 1980s. A new framework is required in which context is a foreground feature and politicians, parents, administrators and groups organized around gender, race and employment interests are significant factors, and examination boards, inspection, forms of accountability and teacher assessment are structurally prominent features.

This reader offers a small contribution to considerations of curriculum and assessment policy. The articles are a resource for one section of the Open University *Policy-making in Education* course and as such offer only a partial discussion of the features relevant to any contemporary analysis of curriculum and assessment. Important policy issues relating to race and gender appear elsewhere in the course and readers, as do the education and training of 16–19-year-olds, relationships between the education system and work system and the Technical and Vocational Education Initiative.

Turning now to the articles in this reader, Salter and Tapper in the first reading argue that the Great Debate was a device orchestrated by the DES. It enabled the department to erode the decentralized power of teachers and, by its promotion of an economic ideology of education, to win support and render legitimate greater power for the DES. The second reading, from a House of Commons Committee Report, reviews a series of publications following the Great Debate. It strongly criticizes the quality and level of discussion in DES pronouncements on the curriculum, comparing them adversely with the Munn Report on curriculum policy for Scottish secondary schools and with HMI documents. It serves to remind us that the curriculum is more than a collection of subjects and identifies competing principles in the design of curriculum.

The third reading takes the rise and fall of pupil numbers and the level of financial support as important 'logistical' features. These features, Richards argues, will affect the responses that teachers will make to curriculum issues. Richards' consideration of the issues for primary schools in the 1980s assumes an 'increasing pressure from the DES, from HMI and from local education authorities to devise intellectually challenging curricula' going beyond the basic skills. He goes on to discuss three areas—science, craft, design and technology, and mathematics—which are likely to be 'the focus for considerable activity during the next few years'.

Marten Shipman, in the fourth reading, assesses the influence of LEAs on curriculum policy. He argues that their power and influence have been consistently undervalued in the curriculum literature and in the debate over the control of the curriculum. Following a detailed analysis of reactive policy, in response to national pressures and to school-based initiatives, and proactive responses, illustrated by accounts of curriculum initiatives in Coventry and the ILEA, he concludes that it is the way in which LEAs function politically that provides the key to understanding their curriculum policy-making activities.

Local authority influences on the curriculum are also the subject of the extract from the ILEA *Improving Secondary Schools.* This report was initiated by the elected members of ILEA who charged a committee of inquiry with considering the curriculum and organization of ILEA secondary schools, with special reference to pupils who are underachieving, and to pay particular attention to working-class pupils. It is then an example of proactive curriculum policy at the local level. The report itself, however, demonstrates two other aspects of Shipman's analysis in the earlier reading. First, it shows how national concerns, notably as stated by the DES and HMI, influence local policy. Secondly, through the examples of 'good practice' included in the report and recommendations (but not in the extract used), it illustrates how teachers can influence policy-making.

David Raffe reminds readers that, no matter what the intentions of policy-makers may be, it is individuals who decide what programmes of study they will follow. He argues that policies frequently fail to achieve their objectives because their attention focuses around *content*, whereas individual decisions on what options or courses to follow reflect judgements about *context* which are often directly or indirectly concerned with vocational prospects. The preoccupation of policy with curriculum content is thus misplaced.

The last three readings are concerned with assessment and selection. Ranson examines the DES's drive to vocationalize the curriculum and the use of the examination system as a mechanism for control. The link is explicitly made by a senior DES official interviewed during Ranson's research: 'If we can achieve things with the new 17+ examination that will give us an important lever to vocationalize or re-vocationalize the last years of public schooling.'

In the following paper Desmond Nuttall traces the development of a common examinations system at 16+ and discusses the aims and motives of those seeking reform. He argues that the DES's support for national criteria for syllabuses and schemes of assessment, which the DES effectively controls, arose from the desire to curtail curriculum diversity and teacher autonomy. Moreover, Nuttall suggests, the reforms will seriously reduce the ability of the new system to meet contemporary needs either in curriculum (relevance) terms or modes of assessment (the use of profiles and graded tests).

The final reading evaluates the work of the Assessment of Performance Unit (APU). Of particular interest in Caroline Gipps's analysis are the changes in the role and tasks of the APU over time as the DES has developed other mechanisms of control over assessment and curriculum. She concludes that the APU has not usefully contributed to policy-making but that its test developments have considerable potential for alerting teachers to weaknesses in teaching methods and content.

REFERENCES

Butler, R.A. (1971) *The Art of the Possible*, Hamish Hamilton, London.
Education (1976) AEC Conference, 2 July, p. 9.
H.M. Inspectorate (1981) *Curriculum 11–16: review of progress: a joint study by HMI and five LEAS*, HMSO, London.
Kogan, M. (1971) *The Politics of Education*, Penguin, Harmondsworth.
Maclure, S. (1984) Address given at Standing Conference on Studies in Education, 14 December.
Methven, J. (1976) What industry wants, *Times Educational Supplement*, 29 October.
OECD (1975) *Educational Development Strategy in England and Wales*, OECD, Paris.
Shipman, M. (1981) The school curriculum in England, 1970–1990, *Compare*, Volume 11, No. 1, pp. 21–32.

1

The Great Debate
making an ideology

BRIAN SALTER and TED TAPPER

MAKING AN IDEOLOGY—BACKGROUND

The 'natural' ideology of the DES is embedded in its decision-making and planning procedures, its search for the optimum rational mode of operation and the controls it considers necessary for ensuring that its bureaucratic techniques perform efficiently. But to the outsider, who perceives the Department as an institution which should be concerned primarily with educational issues rather than with bureaucratic niceties, it is not a 'natural' ideology. Thus the Expenditure Committee (Tenth Report, 1976, p. xxi) criticized the DES for an over-emphasis on resource allocation, quoting the DES's own evidence which stated that 'DES planning, as undertaken by the Departmental Planning Organization . . . is . . . resource-oriented, being concerned primarily with options of scale, organization and cost *rather than educational content*' [our stress]. Unimpressed by this preoccupation, the committee recommended (ibid.) that the 'DPO should make arrangements for *broader educational objectives* to be kept under review as regularly as the resource implications of objectives through the Public Expenditure Surveys' [our stress]. The lesson to be drawn from this is that what makes sense to a bureaucracy does not necessarily make sense to the audience it is supposed to serve. To justify itself, to endow itself with authority, the Department is obliged to translate its bureaucratic needs into the language and ideas of education. It could not expect its requirements for more efficient resource manipulation within, and more influence over the education system, to carry

Source: From Salter, B. and Tapper, T. (1981) *Education, Politics and the State*, Grant McIntyre, London.

much political weight if expressed literally: the capacity to manage the system had to be given legitimacy under the cloak of educational ideology.

It would be doing the DES an injustice to maintain that it was entirely a novice in the art of ideology promotion. In *Education and the Political Order* (Tapper and Salter, 1978, ch. 7) we have traced the rise of the economic ideology of higher education and demonstrated the convenient links which exist between an ideology which stresses education's role as the servant of the national economy and the output-budgeting planning techniques of the DES. In ideal terms, the individual is portrayed as making rational decisions based on his awareness of employment opportunities to acquire the knowledge and credentials appropriate to his future occupation. This means that the economy gains the manpower it needs, educational planners manage the system in order to produce the appropriate numbers of different vocational outputs and the Robbins principle of educational response to individual demand is conveniently integrated with the principle of educational response to economic demand via the concept of the rational and fully-informed student. However, while it was one thing for the DES to be explicit about higher education's function as servant of the economy, as it was in *Education: A Framework for Expansion* for example (1972, p. 34), it was quite another to apply the same argument to the primary and secondary sectors in a formal and obvious manner and in a short space of time rather than over a number of years. This necessitated a much more total and conscious approach to ideology formation than had been the DES's style in higher education. Higher education had been resistant enough to attempts to erode its autonomy, though the University Grants Committee (UGC) had wilted considerably over the years (see Tapper and Salter, 1978, pp. 168–71), and primary and secondary education were likely to prove even more so. Despite this, in June 1976, four months before Mr Callaghan's speech, we find Mr James Hamilton, Permanent Secretary at the DES, saying to the annual conference of the Association of Education Committees: 'I believe that the so-called secret garden of the curriculum cannot be allowed to remain so secret after all, and that the key to the door must be found and turned' (Devlin and Warnock 1977, p. 13). Intervention was the intention and was already on the way.

The opportunity for the DES to take the ideological initiative came with the request by the Prime Minister in May 1976 for a memorandum from the then Education Secretary, Fred Mulley, on what he discerned as four major areas of public concern: the basic approach in primary schools to the teaching of the three 'Rs': the curriculum for older children in comprehensives; the exam system; and the problems of 16–19-year-olds who have no prospect of going on to higher education yet who seem ill-equipped even for the jobs they find. This was clearly a broad enough brief to provide a platform for the initial stimulus at the governmental level of a substantial reappraisal of the education system.

The selection of items for inclusion in the supposedly confidential 'Yellow Book', as the memorandum was called, had to take into account the political environment of the day. If the DES was to harness the motley collection of external pressures for change to the direction indicated by its internal dynamic towards greater educational managerialism, the balance had to be struck correctly. It could not commit itself too soon. There was certainly no guarantee that, in initiating a debate on education, it would succeed in establishing an ideology which gave itself more authority. Bearing in mind that the intended audience of the Yellow Book was, at least ostensibly, the higher echelons of government, the document can best be seen as a kite-flying exercise which did not try to develop a detailed ideological position. Themes are raised but not fully elaborated. Hence the diagnosis of the problem includes the standard of basic skills (literacy and numeracy), the balance in the curriculum (is there enough science and maths teaching for the country's needs?), the inadequate supply of maths teachers, the need that 'education and training must be planned in a unified way' and the weakness that 'some teachers and some schools may have overemphasized the importance of preparing boys and girls for their roles in society compared with the need to prepare them for their economic role' (*TES*, 1976, pp. 2–3). The links with the economic ideology of education are clearly present but not fully enunciated.

If the diagnosis of the problem lacks coherence, the proposed solutions do not. They are based firmly on the premise that what is good for the DES and all its works is good for education as a whole: more control is therefore essential. This conviction emerges in a number of recommendations. Firstly, the Yellow Book argues that 'the time has probably come to establish generally accepted principles for the composition of the secondary curriculum for all pupils, that is to say a "core curriculum" '. And it just so happens that HMI is already working on models of such core curricula as well as on particular areas of the curriculum that need attention. Secondly, it is no good centralizing the curriculum if the means are not available to check on the efficiency of this move through the appropriate monitoring arrangements. The report therefore recommends an increase in the work of the APU and the acceleration of its programme. Thirdly, it is no good monitoring the system and its deficiencies if the means for remedying them are not available: so the report maintains that HMI's involvement in both initial and inservice teacher training should be strengthened. Fourthly, the vital control from the Department's immediate point of view is the financial one. Several times the report contrasts its own position regarding financial controls with that of the Training Services Agency (TSA) of the Manpower Services Commission (MSC), in their mutual efforts to help the 16 to 19 age group. 'At present', it says 'there is some risk of distortion [of the relationship] because the existing statutory and administrative provisions make it much easier for MSC and TSA than for DES to channel resources quickly and selectively where they are needed.' Consequently, 'if the Department is to play as constructive a role as it could wish, then serious thought needs to be given to some extension of its powers in this direction' (ibid.). To put it another way, give us the tools and we will finish the job.

As an internal government document the Yellow Book did not need to have a well-developed public face and could afford to concentrate on what it regarded as the key issues without too many educational ideological trimmings. For that reason, its importance for us lies in the attention it gives to the capacity to *manage* educational change rather than to the *content* of educational change. Explicit in it is the notion that change can no longer be allowed to occur in a random, disorganized fashion: education must be controlled for its own good. Given this emphasis, it is amusing to note this protestation of innocence from HMI: 'No exercise of power is involved in this search for improvement: the Inspectorate, by tradition and by choice, exerts influence by the presentation of evidence and by advice.' Be that as it may, the report was sufficiently aware of the power politics of the situation to raise some of the strategic issues concerning the implementation of its recommendations. In particular it mentioned the problem of securing the acceptance by local authorities of its ideas, the timing of the necessary review of the Schools Council's functions and constitution ('a move may be precipitated by the examination issue'), and the usefulness of an authoritative pronouncement from the Prime Minister which would both suggest that the Department should give a firmer lead on what goes on in schools and refute the argument that no one except teachers has any right to such a say. It concluded: 'The climate for such a declaration on these lines may in fact now be relatively favourable. Nor need there be any inhibition for fear that the Department could not make use of enhanced opportunity to exercise influence over curriculum and teaching methods: the Inspectorate would have a leading role to play in bringing forward ideas in these areas and is ready to fulfil that responsibility' (ibid.).

The 'climate of opinion' may well have been favourable but it was another question altogether as to whether it could be harnessed and directed in a way which suited the DES's need for self-legitimation. The dynamic within the bureaucracy of the Department may have wrought internal changes but how far these changes could be externalized in ideological guise was problematic. The Yellow Book has provided us with clear indications of the direction the Department preferred the debate to take in its own ideological interests and our analysis now will deal with how far that ambition was realized.

MAKING AN IDEOLOGY—CONTENT

If the ideological content of the Great Debate was to be of any use to the DES then it had to serve other interests apart from those of the Department alone. As well as being the expression in educational values of the DES's bureaucratic needs, it had to assist the aspirations of other powerful groups. Otherwise the Department was likely to find itself ideologically isolated with no possibility of ideological overlap and alliances. For this reason therefore, and because it had already been tested in the field of higher education, the economic ideology of education was a prime candidate. Not only had it already demonstrated its ready ability to be integrated with the quantitative, output—budgeting techniques coming into vogue in the Department but it also provided what was rapidly becoming an essential defence against competition from the MSC. Set up in 1974 to oversee the work of the Employment Services Agency (ESA) and the TSA, the MSC was increasingly presenting itself as the organization with the answers so far as the training needs of the nation were concerned: a not unuseful claim in a period of mounting youth unemployment. Obviously this placed it in direct competition with the traditional training role of the further education sector though this competition was mitigated somewhat by the MSC's need for further education to run courses on its behalf. So an ideology which emphasized education's responsiveness to the economic needs of the nation would clearly afford the DES both protection from the encroachments of the MSC as well as a strong platform for launching co-operative ventures. In addition, and not to be underestimated, the ideology guaranteed the backing of both employers and trade unions.

We have argued elsewhere that for an aspiring educational ideology to be able to mount a serious challenge at the national level it has to link three concepts coherently together: the desired society, the type or types of educated individual necessary for that society, and the educational means required to fulfil these two ends. Now although most of the elements of an economic ideology of education capable of meeting these three criteria had been around for decades, they had never before been brought together in the crucible of an officially sponsored debate. Here was the opportunity to forge permanent links between them. The desired society of the economic ideology is a more rationalized and efficient version of the industrialized society we have already. As the influential government White Paper *An Approach to Industrial Strategy* (frequently referred to in subsequent DES publications) pointed out in 1975, a high wage, high output, high employment economy requires that industrial objectives 'be given priority over other policy aims, and that policy in other areas, *including education,* will need to be influenced by our industrial needs' (DI, 1977, p. 2; our stress), particularly in an era of economic stagnation. Such a society cannot operate successfully without appropriate supporting values and their associated status systems: applied and more vocational skills are upgraded to promote a technical culture with the esteem it already holds in continental society (ibid., pp. 1–2). Elite groups are defined much more in terms of their managerial and professional expertise acquired through a rational and explicit career hierarchy of training and credentialling rather than in terms of more informal criteria.

The individuals necessary for this desired society must accept that education's purpose is primarily to prepare them for their economic role. Mr Callaghan (1976, p. 72) made this point in his Ruskin speech when he argued: 'There is no virtue in [education] producing socially well adjusted members of society who are unemployed because they do not have the skills.' (Though, to be fair, he continued: 'Nor at the other extreme must they be technically efficient robots.') At the more sophisticated end of the scale this means that we have the image of rationally economic and educational man moving effortlessly through the education system and gliding into the appropriate (for the economy) industrial niche:

> One aim of school education is to ensure that, as pupils progress through school, they develop an understanding about the role of industry in society, the challenges and breadth of employment it offers and the education and training necessary for a successful industrial career. In this way they can come to a more informed choice about which subjects at school and which discipline to follow in further and higher education. Pupils and their parents need to have the information early enough to ensure that their curricular choices in school will be appropriate for their further education and for the career they wish to follow (DI, 1977, p. 21).

Some have higher niches than others, of course, and for those lower down, this elegant and informed passage through the educational system is not really appropriate. For those less fortunate it is most important to attain the basic standards of literacy and numeracy which many employers claimed, and claim, are lacking in those presently entering the nation's industrial workforce. Nevertheless, what both of these desired products of education have in common is a mutual understanding and acceptance of the contribution that industry makes to the well-being of the country.

Just as the desired society of the economic ideology of education requires a rearrangement of existing status systems to improve the position of professional and technical cultures, so the parallel definitions of educated individuals include particular ideas regarding the types of knowledge they should possess. 'Applied' rather than 'pure' knowledge is preferred though this insistence wavers when it comes to a conflict over whether engineers or scientists best serve the nation's interest partly because the 'pure' scientist lobby of the late 1960s still retained considerable influence in the 1970s (see Garnicot and Blaug, 1973). On the whole, though, the Great Debate saw the new ideology embracing the engineer and technologist, the embodiments of applied knowledge, as its favourite sons. This is illustrated by the UGC's decision in 1977 to promote a small number of very high quality first degree courses in engineering with a pronounced orientation towards manufacturing industry (UGC, 1978).

To a large extent, these first two components of the new ideology (desired society and desired individual characteristics) could be left to their natural sponsors to promote—employers, trade unions, Department of Industry, private interest groups such as the Industry Society, etc. Once the public vehicle for their expression was provided in the form of the Great Debate they could emerge as they had done on numerous occasions in the past. In 1928, for example, the Malcolm Committee produced its report *Education and Industry* to a barrage of complaints in the press and from employers about standards of literacy and numeracy in schools. And in the postwar years the Federation of British Industries (FBI) regularly bemoaned the lack of liaison between education and industry writing at least four reports on the topic in the period up to 1965. Similarly, in more scholarly circles there is a well-established school of thought which attributes Britain's economic decline at least partly to the Victorians' failure to develop the education system essential for national efficiency, comparing us unfavourably with our continental rivals in this respect (see Gowing, 1976; Sanderson, 1972; Simon, 1965, ch. 6). There was no lack of forces prepared to push the first two components once the opportunity arose. However, specifying the educational means necessary for realizing these societal and individual goals of education was a complex task which only the DES itself could undertake. The trick so far as the Department was concerned was to integrate its ambition for more comprehensive lines of educational management with the other two components of the ideology.

In both the background paper for the regional conferences of early 1977, *Educating Our Children* (DES, 1977a), and the Green Paper of July 1977, *Education in Schools* (DES, 1977b), summarizing the results of the Debate and making proposals for the future, many of the ideas contained in the Yellow Book re-emerge—albeit in more diplomatic form. *Educating Our Children* argues for a common core curriculum: the Green Paper echoes this call but within a broader strategic perspective which proposes, first of all, that local authorities carry out a review of curricular arrangements in their own schools. Following on from this,

> They [the Secretaries of State for Education] will in the light of the review seek to establish a broad agreement with their partners in the education service on a framework for the curriculum, and on whether part of the curriculum should be protected because there are aims common to all schools and pupils at certain stages. These aims must include the achievement of basic literacy and numeracy at the primary stage (*TES*, 1977, p. 5).

The subtlety of this statement lies in its implication that the DES is seeking control through co-operation, that it is still in the business of reflecting the educational consensus. As we shall see, the increasing dominance of the Department in terms of both information and value supply in education renders the word 'co-operation' little more than an imaginative political device.

On the question of the most effective means of monitoring an education system geared to economic goals, *Educating Our Children* is less shy about the importance of controlling information flows. Referring to the assessment of standards, it states that the aim is:

to measure, in terms of selected aspects of performance, the effectiveness of the education system as a whole, or local parts of it.... Better information on standards should improve the quality of rationally-based discussion of educational issues; its provision should assist those making policy decisions at central and local government level and also teachers and teacher trainees. At the local level it could help to indicate schools with a particular need for extra measures or help from the local education authority (DES, 1977, p. 7).

Once national or local needs are identified the issue then arises of how they are to be met and, in particular, how the teaching force can best be deployed to meet those needs. Hence it is no surprise to find the Green Paper arguing for more systematic approaches to the recruitment, career development, training and deployment of the teacher force and for more information about it (*TES*, 1977, p. 8).

In terms of the coherence and staying power of the economic ideology of education, it was important that the educational means for the realization of individual and societal goals should be linked to the latter two components of the ideology: a bare statement of the DES's interventionist intentions would have been impolitic to say the least. This tying together of educational means and economic goals occurred at a number of levels. Within the school it was argued that room should be made for the cultivation of an improved understanding of productive industry and an improved position for careers guidance in the curriculum. 'Local education authorities, schools and industry must work much more closely together', maintained the Green Paper (ibid., p. 8) and continued: 'Industry, the trades unions and commerce should be involved in curriculum planning processes.' Similarly, at the level of teacher training the case was frequently made (ibid., p. 5) that 'more attention should be given ... to the national importance of industry and commerce, to helping them [teachers] in their responsibility for conveying this to their pupils'. The age of the independent teacher, justifying his autonomy and control over the curriculum in terms of his professional competence, was, according to this line of reasoning, at an end.

WHAT GREAT DEBATE?

In conclusion we deal first with the view expressed by the more sceptical observers that the Great Debate was not 'really' a debate, that it was stage-managed in order to exclude certain policy options, that most of the participants sooner or later realized what they were doing and considered the process a sterile one, and that therefore the whole thing was a contrivance and cannot be taken seriously. Apart from the final deduction, we would not disagree with this view. What we deduce instead is that the significance of the Great Debate lies precisely in the fact that individuals participated knowing that it was a contrivance. And the reason they had to participate was that the DES had succeeded in giving the Great Debate the status of an ideological forum where certain battles about the condition and future of education should be fought out. That it was not a fair and balanced exchange of views by rational individuals is of little consequence to its long-term political impact. What is of consequence is that the main educational interests felt obliged to take part, that it was highly visible and that at the public level at least most participants played the game and appeared to take it seriously. That was really all that the Department wanted and, at that point, needed.

The Department needed the debate because the bureaucratization of educational power could not continue under the reigning ideological conditions. If the Department was to increase both its own and local authorities' capacity to manage educational change then a renegotiation of the prevalent educational ideology had to take place. At the same time external economic pressures complemented the internal bureaucratic dynamic by insisting that, in a time of crisis, education should become accountable to the economy. Such accountability could not be achieved, the DES argued, without the introduction of new lines of management planning and control. We have described the ideological result of the harnessing of the economic pressures by the bureaucratic dynamic as the new economic ideology of education. It is an ideology which, if successfully implemented, conveniently legitimizes the ambitions of national and local bureaucracies for more rational means of organizing the education system. The vital questions, of course, are: how far has the new ideology already been implemented (i.e. become authoritative), and what are its chances for success in the future? In that the Great Debate signalled the public unveiling of the new educational ideology, the first steps in its implementation cannot be said to have gone too badly. A procession of documents established the main tenets of the ideology with only token resistance being met from opponents who were largely outgunned and outmanoeuvred. The requisite organizational adjustments to support the new ideology were already in train and continued during and after the Great Debate. Indeed, it was noticeable how the debate effectively paved the way for the expanded HMI and APU activities. If the bureaucratization of educational power is to continue, so also must the process of its legitimation through the appropriate ideological reinforcement. For that reason it is unlikely that we have seen the last of the Great Debate format for the public airing of educational issues by the DES. Until the Department's own organic intellectuals can assume an easy dominance of educational ideas, the elaboration and restating of the new educational ideology must take place on an open and public basis.

REFERENCES

Callaghan, J. (1976) Ruskin speech. *Times Educational Supplement*, 22 October, p. 72.

(DES) Department of Education and Science (1972) *Education: A Framework for Expansion*, HMSO, London.

(DES) Department of Education and Science (1977a) *Educating our Children—Four Subjects for Debate*, HMSO, London.

(DES) Department of Education and Science (1977b) *Education in Schools. A Consultative Document* (Cmnd 6869), HMSO, London.

(DI) Department of Industry (1977) *Industry, Education and Management, a Discussion Paper*, HMSO, London.

Devlin, T. and Warnock, M. (1977) *What Must We Teach?* Maurice Temple Smith, London.

Fowler, G., Morris, V. and Ozga, J. (eds.) (1973) *Decision-making in British Education.* Heinemann, London.

Garnicot, K.G. and Blaug, M. (1973) Manpower forecasting since Robbins—a science lobby in action. In G. Fowler *et al.* (eds.) (1973).

Gowing, M. (1976) Lost opportunities in an age of imperialism. *Times Higher Educational Supplement*, 26 November, p. 15.

Sanderson, M. (1972) *The Universities and British Industry*, Routledge & Kegan Paul, London.

Simon, B. (1965) *Studies in the History of Education and the Labour Movement, 1870-1920*, Lawrence & Wishart, London.

(TES) Times Educational Supplement (1976) Extracts from the Yellow Book, 15 October, pp. 2-3.

(TES) Times Educational Supplement (1977) Extracts from the Green Paper, 22 July, pp. 5, 8.

Tapper, T. and Salter, B. (1978) *Education and the Political Order*, Macmillan, London.

Tenth Report from the Expenditure Committee (1976) *Policy-making in the DES* (Sessions 1975-76, Cmnd 6678), HMSO, London.

(UGC) University Grants Committee (1978) Annual Survey 1976-77 (Cmnd 7119), HMSO, London.

2

The Secondary School Curriculum and Examinations

HOUSE OF COMMONS EDUCATION, SCIENCE AND ARTS COMMITTEE

[The Education, Science and Arts Committee is appointed to examine the expenditure, administration and policy of the Department of Education and Science and associated bodies. It has power to send for persons, papers and records; it may appoint persons with technical knowledge to assist in its work.]

2.1. Through the mass of the evidence we have received it is, in our view, too easy to lose sight of what education should be for. We believe it is important for us to give our view. One piece of evidence quoted the statement of aims which was recently put forward by the Warnock committee. The aims, the committee said, were 'first to enlarge a child's knowledge, experience and imaginative understanding, and thus his (or her) awareness of moral values and capacity for enjoyment; and secondly to enable him (or her) to enter the world after formal education is over as an active participant in society and a responsible contributor to it, capable of achieving as much independence as possible'.[1] We endorse this statement, but we would want to elaborate on it in three respects.

2.2. First, we need to consider the way in which these aims can be achieved. We entirely endorse the Munn committee's view that education is not the same as the 'formal' curriculum.[2] 'Education' is a much wider process, involving relationships, values, and experiences. There should of course be a considerable degree of relationship between the formal curriculum and these processes, but they are not, in logic or in practice, the same thing. It looked at one time in the recent discussions on the curriculum that the particular kind of emphasis which the DES placed ran the risk of divorcing the formal

Source: From *The Secondary School Curriculum and Examinations*, House of Commons Education, Science and Art Committee, Second Report Session 1981–2, Vol. 1, HMSO, London.

curriculum from the 'informal' and 'hidden' curricula. Any such divorce would be short-sighted and counterproductive. In framing this report we have borne in mind the needs of individual pupils in his or her experiences both inside and outside the classroom.

2.3. Second, it is important to consider the means by which the appropriate balances can be altered in response to changing circumstances. One of the most powerful arguments against a centrally controlled curriculum is that it is inflexible, both in relation to changes in society at large and to local and regional circumstances. We cannot afford to burden individual schools and teachers with bureaucratic mechanisms, which would be both professionally debilitating and insufficiently sensitive to the needs of pupils. We are strongly in favour, for example, of the recent provision of the Education Act 1980 that parents and teachers should be members of all governing bodies. We are convinced that the involvement of the local community, and especially parents, is the most effective means of ensuring not simply a satisfactory curriculum provision, but also of securing continuities between the values and practices of the schools, the family, and the world of employment.

2.4. Finally, we believe that we must relate the values of schools to those which govern society at large. Of course, young people must be given the intellectual and moral means to be critical of that society and should not be expected to accept things as they are, and tolerance of diversity is in any case one of the values which most people would wish to transmit to a new generation. At the same time, we believe that both schools and families have to be positive in their attitude towards these matters, and must beware of assuming that the values can be acquired without specific attention being given to their realization and comprehension. It is not the least important aspect of the stress we place on the closer relation between schools and the outside world, especially the family, that it may serve to reinforce this important process. It appears to us that this is an aspect of the curriculum (in its widest sense) which may have been neglected over the past few years. The consequences of any such neglect may be serious and long term.

2.5. The education system at present distributes powers and responsibilities widely among the various parties concerned. The formal position was summarized for us by the Department of Education and Science (DES) in written evidence:

> Section 1 of the 1944 Education Act places a general duty on the Secretary of State to promote the education of the people; Section 8 requires every local education authority to 'secure that there shall be available for their area sufficient schools for providing primary . . . and . . . secondary education, "offering for all pupils", such variety of instruction and training as may be desirable in view of their different ages, abilities and aptitudes'. Section 23 of the Education Act 1944 provides that . . . the local education authority shall control the secular instruction in all schools except voluntary aided secondary schools . . . The model articles for county schools, adopted in 1945, provide that the

authority shall determine the general educational character of the school and its place in the local educational system and that, subject to this, the governors shall have the general direction of the conduct and curriculum. In practice, curricular matters are devolved to the head teacher and his staff.

We quote the DES summary, though there is one point which deserves comment. In summarizing the position the DES have omitted a rather important passage of Section 1 of the 1944 Act. It is certainly true that Section 1 places a general duty on the Secretary of State to promote the education of the people. But it also places on him the duty to 'secure the effective execution by local authorities, under his control and direction, of the national policy for providing a varied and comprehensive educational service in each area'.

2.6. In the broadest terms, the Act envisages four principal ways in which the Secretary of State could operate in order to fulfil his duties so far as the curriculum is concerned. Section 4 provided that 'There shall be two Central Advisory Councils for Education, one for England and the other for Wales'. Although the General Certificate of Education (GCE) examination boards are autonomous bodies, the Secretary of State also has some powers, some formal and some informal, over the examination system. The mechanism of Her Majesty's Inspectorate is also available to him, though the degree to which this body is responsible to the Secretary of State was, and remains, a somewhat cloudy issue. He is, finally, given residual powers, applicable to the curriculum as to other aspects of the system, to intervene where it appeared to him that LEAs or governors were acting unreasonably in respect of any power or duty or were failing to fulfil their duties. Sections 11 and 12 of the 1944 Act empowered the Secretary of State to call for plans from local authorities. In fact, the Central Advisory Councils (CAC) have not been appointed for over ten years, in spite of the Act's statement that such bodies shall exist, and Sections 11 and 12 of the Act have recently been repealed.

2.7. The system envisages that the Secretary of State would in general only have *influence* over the curriculum, and that this influence should be mediated by a series of mechanisms, each of which enjoys a measure of independence from political control. The Secondary Schools Examination Council until 1963 (when most of its functions were taken over by the Schools Council) approved all GCE O and A Level syllabuses, but it was dominated by teachers and the LEAs, with the major Departmental influence being through Her Majesty's Inspectors. The Schools Council itself was widely felt, prior at least to its reconstitution in 1977, to be dominated by teachers, and specifically by the teacher unions. Although it is well established that the Secretary of State may give directions to HMI, the professional autonomy of that body is prized. Similarly, while the Central Advisory Councils were appointed by the Secretary of State, there was no suggestion that he was in a position to influence their conclusions directly, or to prevent them publishing their views.

2.8. One effect of this devolved pattern is that it enhances the autonomy of individual heads and teachers. In practice, curricular matters are generally devolved to the head teacher and staff. The head's freedom is subject to a variety of influences and constraints, but on the whole these affect the pattern of subject offerings and content rather than method. In the latter area, teachers have considerable freedom, and the way in which it is exercised is often unknown outside the individual school. This freedom, unusual in Western European countries, is by now both cherished and traditional and probably explains the reluctance of governments since 1944 to make other than very general statements of aims and hopes for the curriculum.

. . . .

2.10. Recently, there has been a considerable increase in the DES interest in the curriculum. The Assessment of Performance Unit, wholly within the DES, was set up in 1974, and is charged with monitoring the performance of primary and secondary schools in several key areas. Following the then Prime Minister's speech at Ruskin College, Oxford, in 1976, a review of the constitution of the Schools Council was undertaken which resulted in a reduction in the representation of teachers on several key committees. Meanwhile the Secretary of State instituted a series of extensive public discussions on the curriculum, which was to culminate in the publication of *The School Curriculum* document under the new administration. The DES has also taken a very positive and leading role in the arrangements for a new system of examining at 16+, and has to some degree moved back into a role which was originally delegated to the Schools Council.[3]

2.11. This combination of circumstances make the current historical moment one of considerable importance for the future of our educational system. Over the past five years, virtually every public body and grouping has published its views on the curriculum and there is now a formidable selection of documents, including several from HMI and the Schools Council. This report, therefore, is written in the light of knowledge and views of a wide number of experts and organisations within and without the educational world. It is written at a time of growing expectation, of growing concern at the number of problems in the late twentieth century to which the schools must provide part of the solution. Yet it is written at a time of diminishing resources and in the knowledge that the present system leaves every school in the land to respond to any curricular change as it sees fit: a system which makes it impossible for any national body, Parliament or Government to know the totality and the detail of what is being offered to the nation's children in the years before most of them will be seeking employment.

THE CURRICULUM AND 'THE SCHOOL CURRICULUM'

Debate and context

3.1. The publication by the department of state responsible for education of a national statement about what should be offered and experienced in our schools is, by any account, a major event. One might expect to find much in such a statement to ponder as a means of discovering more about us and our time, about our particular strengths, weaknesses and predilections, and about how we see ourselves adapting to the major changes which are occurring in all advanced industrial countries at this time.

3.2. The first noteworthy feature of *The School Curriculum* is perhaps the way it was produced. It has not been written by a group of experienced professionals, as was the case in Scotland, where a committee of educationalists was set the task under the chairmanship of the Rector of a High School.[4] This document has instead been drafted by departmental civil servants and merely modified in discussion with other interested, official parties.

3.3. It may also be pertinent to ask why such a document has been thought necessary. An event of this kind is worthy of analysis in a nation which, unlike most others, has not found a national statement on the curriculum necessary during a hundred and more years of development. The evidence on this point could be regarded as conflicting. On the one hand there are those who say that it is quite unnecessary, that anything of importance in such a document is being done by schools anyway, or that, even if it is not, this is an inefficient way of going about it. The strength of a devolved system, such arguments go, resides in the level of commitment on the part of those who have to implement a curriculum. Others, not noticeably of an interventionist persuasion, will say that schools have changed too much or too fast, without due consideration for the consequences of the changes and without due regard to the balance of the curriculum offering which results. Those who tend towards such a viewpoint will point to the proliferation both of 'new' subjects, and the proliferation of syllabuses in 'old' ones, together with the loss of an integrated sense of *purpose* in the work of schools which, it is said, has resulted from the fragmentation of traditional patterns. Still others—and a growing number of official bodies take this view—complain that the curriculum has not changed fast enough. Such antagonists will argue that, in place of education for an Empire, England and Wales still do not have a widespread education for Europe, or for the advanced nations' responsibility towards a developing world; they still have not replaced traditional distinctions between intellectual, emotional, moral and practical education with a more integrated ideology; that they still lack a curriculum that recognises the needs and the equality of both sexes; and that they have on the whole failed to adjust what happens in schools to the presence of pupils of varied ethnic and cultural backgrounds.

3.4. Our own view is that there is truth, of some kind and some weight, in all these views, without exception. We found all of them reflected, to some degree, in the evidence we received. Many were concerned that in a system based essentially on a partnership between various parties, nothing should be done which might endanger the existing balance of interests or the sense of involvement and responsibility. Others, like the National Association of Careers and Guidance Teachers (NACGT), complained about the variety of options in the fourth and fifth years, which 'have done little to enhance either the education prospects or the post-school prospects of young people'. Complaints of the excessively academic nature of the traditional curriculum were common and both the Equal Opportunities Commission (EOC) and the Commission for Racial Equality (CRE) clearly regarded much progress as necessary in the schools before true equality of opportunity for girls and minority ethnic groups could be achieved. So far as minority ethnic groups are concerned, the point was underlined during the course of our enquiry by the publication of the Rampton report on the education of children of West Indian origin, by riots and disorder in our inner cities and Lord Scarman's report on these events, and by the Fifth Report from the Home Affairs Committee on *Racial Disadvantage*.[5]

Pursuit of consensus

3.5. It was in pursuit of some consensus on all these matters that the DES began its lengthy series of consultations which has now continued under two successive governments. In the early stages of these consultations, it cannot be said that the DES achieved much success in securing a consensus. Indeed, it sometimes seemed that the nearest to a consensus that was likely was one to the effect that the DES did not understand the problem. The consultative document entitled *A Framework for the School Curriculum*[6] was very widely criticized when it was published in January 1980, and fundamental criticisms were offered by some of the most prominent official bodies in the educational world, such as the Schools Council and the local authority associations.

3.6. The most recent publication, *The School Curriculum*, is a document of an altogether more careful kind. Most of our witnesses were prepared to welcome it, though it sometimes seemed that this was more in a sense of relief at what it did not say than a positive affirmation of what it did. We should say at once that we join in this general welcome. We are particularly glad to see a recognition of the complexity of the issues involved, and a recognition that some areas, such as science and modern languages, require further action at the national level. There is no longer a concern to specify the amount of time which should be devoted to specific subjects (a major source of criticism of the earlier documents), and we heard evidence of a considerable amount of prior consultation at the draft stage. Published soon after the DES document was one from the Schools Council, *The Practical Curriculum*.[7] As participants in the Council, the DES and HMI were also involved in this production, which purports to offer the practical counterpart to the DES document, though as the Chairman of the Council acknowledged in evidence the meshing of the two 'requires a rather sophisticated gearbox'. Taken together with three HMI documents,[8] we now have a complete set from all the relevant national, official bodies.

3.7. One of the most widespread criticisms of previous DES utterances concerned the emphasis on subjects. *The School Curriculum* qualifies this approach as follows:

> The Secretaries of State recognise that the curriculum can be described and analysed in several ways, each of which has its advantages and limitations. They have thought it most helpful to express much of their guidance in terms of subjects, because secondary school timetables are almost always devised in subject terms, they are readily recognised by parents and employers, and most secondary school teachers are trained in subjects. But a subject title hardly indicates the content or level of study, or the extent to which teaching and learning meet particular objectives. Moreover, many important elements of the curriculum are to be found 'across the curriculum' rather than exclusively within any one subject. A subject title is a kind of shorthand, whose real educational meaning depends on the school's definition of what it expects children will learn and be able to do as a result of their studies in the subject in question. Some subjects contribute to more than one aim of the curriculum; some aims need a contribution from more than one subject. In analysing the curriculum, therefore, other frames of reference are also required. These may be in terms of the skills required at particular stages of a pupil's career; or of areas of experience such as the eight used in HM Inspector's working papers on the 11-16 curriculum: the aesthetic and creative, the ethical, the linguistic, the mathematical, the physical, the scientific, the social and political, and the spiritual. In translating general principles into practice schools need to develop more than one kind of analysis as working tools of curriculum planning (para 19).

A similar justification is used by the Schools Council in *The Practical Curriculum*:

> A realistic discussion of what is taught in schools needs to start from where we are, not where we might or ought to be. Schools for young children usually organise their work through class teachers: older pupils tend to organise their work through subject departments. Subjects are therefore a natural entry to the curriculum of a secondary school. In practice many teachers of young children also seem to find it helpful to think about their work in terms of subjects (page 13).

This approach can be contrasted with that adopted by HMI in their *Curriculum 11-16* document. The analysis there consists of a philosophical description of 'areas of experience'. *The School Curriculum* gives a mention of the HMI analysis, and the Schools Council adds one towards the well known 'forms of knowledge' analysis proposed by Hirst and Peters[9] and a different framework proposed by Lawton.[10]

3.8. To those objectors who complained that the DES did not appear to appreciate that *how* things were taught is just as important as *what* is taught, the document now says that 'In the day-to-day work of schools, what is taught and how it is taught are in practice inseparable '.[11] As for those who are concerned that themes treated 'across the curriculum' may be understated or ignored by the subject approach, they can rest assured that there are 'some essential constituents of the school curriculum which are often identified as subjects but which are as likely to feature in a variety of courses and programmes and may be more effectively covered if they are distributed across the curriculum'.[12] If one is concerned that several crucial elements in a modern curriculum can be glossed over by the use of the shorthand of 'subjects', then the alert reader can find an admonition to the effect that 'the work of schools has to reflect many issues with which pupils will have to come to terms as they mature, and,' the document continues, 'schools and teachers are familiar with them.'[13] In this way the document seeks to deal, in one brief paragraph, with the multi-cultural nature of society, the effect of technology on employment patterns, the equality of the sexes.

3.9. Between the publication of *A Framework for the Curriculum* in 1977 and *The School Curriculum* in 1981, the DES philosophy does not seem to have changed significantly. We may contrast the approach of the Munn[14] and Dunning[15] Reports which undertook a parallel exercise for the Scottish system. Chapter 3 of the Munn report begins by frankly confessing the scale of the problem:

> All curriculum design must start from fundamental principles, which are themselves, inevitably, matters of debate. What educational aims should the schools set themselves? What human capacities should they try to foster? What kinds of knowledge are of most worth? These are the perennial questions for curriculum designers; and over the years teachers, philosophers, psychologists, industrialists, educational theorists, defenders of tradition, revolutionaries and others have offered very different answers. The curricula adopted have usually represented attempts to reconcile some, if not all, of the conflicting views then current in society; and this points to the nature of the problem we ourselves are faced with. We are very conscious that our own review of the curriculum takes place at a time when the diversity of the demands made on schools is unprecedented, and when the curriculum itself has become a battleground for conflicting ideologies and competing claims. In this chapter we attempt to identify and analyse these various pressures, since it is through them that the curriculum of the future must be forged.

To compare the DES and Munn reports may not seem entirely fair; but it must be realised that both are official government documents. The difference in approach is that the Munn report considers that the wealth of public discussion, and the various pressures on the schools, are the *starting point* of a proper analysis, and are not to be deflected into occasional qualifying paragraphs. The chapter from which we have quoted continues by exploring the appropriate relationship between schools and society, the relationship between the demands of society and the needs of individual pupils, the accountability of schools, and the difficulties which schools encounter when they begin to try to adjudicate between conflicting demands and pressures. It continues to classify these 'claims' on the curriculum as composed of three sets: the 'social', the 'epistemological' ('theories on the nature of knowledge') and the 'psychological' ('based on the psychology of the pupils themselves'). In the view of the Munn committee any adequate curriculum must satisfy all three of these 'claims', subject of course to practicality and the support of those who will be expected to implement it. The committee was also extremely anxious to stress that it did not regard the 'hidden' curriculum ('the whole ethos established by the atmosphere of the school') or the 'informal curriculum' ('activities... carried on under the school's auspices but outwith the formal teaching programme') as peripheral to its enquiry. 'All these aspects of the curriculum, we agreed, had vital contributions to make to the education of all pupils.'

Alternative approaches

3.10. Those seeking a more adequate statement than is offered in *The School Curriculum* may be referred to Chapters 3 and 4 of the Munn report. The stress on subjects in the former does not, in our view, lead to an adequate analysis, and the deficiencies are more serious in some areas—for example, the diverse needs of girls and minority ethnic groups—than in others. We shall return to these issues. The approach also leads to a stress on a 'broad' curriculum offering, a matter on which the Munn committee is sceptical.[16] Such an approach also means that insufficient attention is given to the 'informal' and 'hidden' curricula, and to the way in which learning is organized. There is no serious consideration of issues of what HMIs referred to as the 'surrender value' of subjects, which we understand to mean the extent to which pupils may drop some course of study while retaining some lasting benefit, and nothing concerning the effectivess of 'drip-feed' learning as distinct from intensive courses of study. In many areas of the curriculum—we might single out maths and modern languages in particular—it is much more important that schools should decide their policies in terms of the skills to be acquired and then decide what time is necessary.

3.11. Even considered on its own terms, it appears to us that there are deficiencies in the document. Some 'humanities' are recommended and some 'practical' and 'aesthetic' activity, but it is clear that the humanities and the arts have a rather low priority. Discrimination as to *what* humanities, *what* aesthetic and practical activity, are apparently minor considerations which can safely be left vague. We have found a general ambiguity about the humanities and arts which we feel should be regretted. In paragraph 22 *The School Curriculum* speaks of the 'breadth' of the curriculum:

> History, geography and economics serve to give the pupil an insight into the nature of society (including his own) and man's place in his environment. Classical languages introduce the pupil to aspects of history and culture as well as the disciplines of language and literature.

We regard this kind of statement as precisely of the kind which government (or for that matter any informed person) should avoid. To begin with, the lumping together of such different subject areas as 'history, geography and economics', as if they were in some way interchangeable, does no service to education nor to the credibility of the authors. We note, too, the phrasing of the statement: these subjects 'serve' (not *'can* serve'), classical languages 'introduce' (not *'can* introduce'). As evidence to the Committee indicated, there is no necessary connection between the teaching of these subjects and these effects, at all. Nor are these the only insights which might be singled out: without going at all deeply into the matter we might point to cultural heritage, the application of mathematical method to human behaviour, and an empathetic awareness of remote cultures. If it is objected that all these things are encompassed in the phrase 'nature of society', then we can only say that in that case we regard the phrase as vacuous and unhelpful. We might note here that, although English is given a high priority, it is almost entirely in terms of language skills; the reader will search in vain for a proper emphasis on the humanizing influence of the study of literature. As for the point about classical languages, it is necessary to observe that two distinct senses of the word 'discipline' are here confused, and confused in a way which, given the context, many will find disturbing. 'Language and literature' can be disciplines in the sense of being subject areas in their own right. They can also be disciplines in the more elementary sense of involving a great deal of hard work and application. A clearer distinction should have been made.

3.12. The same paragraph continues:

> Subjects like art, music and drama are needed to develop sensibilities without which the pupil will not be able to avail himself of many opportunities for enriching his personal experience. Such subjects as physical education, home economics and craft, design and technology make a particular contribution to the acquisition of physical and practical skills which are an essential complement of the pupil's intellectual and personal development (para 22).

We suggest that it is not necessary to be a strong proponent of creative aspects of the curriculum to consider this description of their potential role as essentially dismissive and lacking in any sympathetic awareness either of the schools or of pupils' personal development. Evidence received by the Committee from the Gulbenkian Foundation, for example, summarized a forthcoming report commissioned by the Foundation and referred to the role of the arts in the following areas:

In developing the full variety of human intelligence and capabilities
In developing the ability for creative thought and action
In the education of feeling and sensibility
In the exploration of values
In the understanding cultural change
In developing physical and perceptual skills.

Meanwhile we received evidence from many bodies concerned with 'practical' areas of the curriculum, such as the Royal Society of Arts, to the effect that the distinction between 'physical and practical' on the one hand and 'intellectual and personal' on the other was dangerous and fallacious, and moreover that the continuing maintenance of such distinctions was one of the most serious short-comings in our educational system.

3.13. We have already referred to several other official documents, two of which deserve brief mention. The Schools Council's *Practical Curriculum* purports to offer a more detailed set of guidance and suggestions for those who are actually involved in curriculum planning. The technique is to scatter a wealth of differing, but nevertheless viable, solutions as examples which can be set aside or taken up by practitioners. As an aid to this process, teachers are offered a bewildering number of checklists of one kind or another. One assiduous reviewer has counted 25 in all. There are some signs that the range of alternatives owes rather more to a concern to encompass different views within the Council than to a considered diversity: there are inconsistencies and evidence here and there of haste. Nevertheless, the ultimate test of a practical document is whether practitioners find it of practical use. We have some doubts about this, though we welcome the attempt.

3.14. The HMI 'red book', *Curriculum 11–16*, is a more thoughtful document,[17] and its proposal that the curriculum should be analysed by using a set of 'areas of experience' is probably the most coherent proposal so far, and a rather more hopeful framework for development than *A View of the Curriculum*, which was published three years later in 1980.[18] The recent follow-up to *Curriculum 11–16* reports on progress with detailed work in five local authorities on the original document.[19] The results are encouraging: the schools which took part in the exercise have certainly benefited and have been encouraged to examine their curriculum offerings with a seriousness and thoughtfulness which would otherwise have been unlikely. It is not always clear, however, how far this progress derives from the 'areas of experience' analysis. The reader is occasionally left wondering whether the results of such an intensive exercise would not have been rather similar if the original document had not been available.

3.15. We believe that schools should regard the provisions of *The School Curriculum* with some scepticism. It is in many respects a confused document, lacking in intellectual distinction and practicality alike. Many have doubted the DES's competence in the area of the curriculum, and this document, together with its associated Circular 6/81, will do nothing to dispel these doubts. We have already recorded our view that Scotland has come rather better out of the national curriculum debate than England and Wales, and that HMI's *Curriculum 11–16* provides a better framework for analysis than anything in *The School Curriculum*. We hope that, in responding to Circular 6/81, schools will take all these documents into account in framing their curricular aims. We may add that, in default of a better account, it appears to us that responsible heads and teachers may prove more effective with a combination of common sense and close consultation with local interests and parents than they would by a close adherence to these guidelines.

NOTES AND REFERENCES

1. Evidence, p. 474 (written evidence presented to the Committee).
2. See below, paras. 3.2 and 3.9.
3. The Schools Council was closed in 1982.

4. Scottish Education Department, *The Structure of the Curriculum in the Third and Fourth Years of the Scottish Secondary School*, HMSO, Edinburgh: 1977. (The 'Munn Report'.)
5. *West Indian Children in Our Schools: Interim Report of the Committee of Enquiry into the Education of Children from Minority Ethnic Groups*, HMSO, London: 1981. *Brixton Disorders 10–12 April 1981*, Cmnd 8427. *Racial Disadvantage*, Fifth Report from the Home Affairs Committee, Session 1980–81, HC 424–1, HMSO, London, 1981.
6. DES and Welsh Office.
7. Schools Council Working Paper 70, Methuen Educational 1981.
8. HMI, *Curriculum 11–16*, HMSO, London: 1977. HMI, *A View of the Curriculum*, HMSO, London: 1980. HMI, *Curriculum 11–16, A Review of Progress*, HMSO, London: 1981.
9. P.H. Hirst and R.S. Peters, *The Logic of Education*, Routledge, London: 1970.
10. D. Lawton, *Social Change, Educational Theory and Curriculum Planning*, University of London Press, London: 1973.
11. *The School Curriculum*, para. 30.
12. Ibid., para. 23.
13. Ibid., para. 21.
14. Op. cit.
15. *Assessment for All. Report of the Committee to Review Assessment in the Third and Fourth Years of Secondary Education in Scotland*, HMSO, Scottish Education Department: 1977.
16. We found in our enquiry that phrases like 'the broad curriculum' and 'balanced offering' were used in rather different ways by many of our witnesses. For some 'broad' appeared to mean the offering of as wide a range of subject options as possible, while others used it in a more general sense to mean the avoidance of excessive or premature specialization. The Munn report's scepticism on the matter seems directed at the first sense. Our own support for a 'broad' curriculum later in this report is in the second sense, and derives from our concern that the 14 to 16 curriculum should leave as many doors open as possible.
17. HMI, *Curriculum 11–16*, HMSO, London: 1977, 'The Red Book'.
18. HMI, *A View of the Curriculum*, HMSO, London: 1980.
19. HMI, *Curriculum 11–16, A Review of Progress*, HMSO, London: 1981.

3

Utopia Deferred
curriculum issues for primary and middle school education

COLIN RICHARDS

Compared with 1973, when the first Standing Conference on Curriculum Studies was held in Exeter, discussion about the primary curriculum and its possible development can now take place on a more informed, less conjectural basis. As a result of surveys (DES, 1978, 1980; DENI, 1981) and other researches (e.g. Galton, Simon and Croll, 1980; Bennett *et al.*, 1980; Steadman *et al.*, 1979) we now know much more than we did about the state of primary education generally and about the difficult problems of effecting change in curriculum, pedagogy or evaluation. As a result of a decade of financial and demographic contraction and of dissensus rather than consensus in educational policy making at national and local authority levels, we are less naïve than we were and more aware of the socio-political obstacles in the way of transforming schools or the wider society. Greater self-knowledge has brought with it an inevitable sense of discomfort; greater political awareness has brought with it an acknowledgement of the fragility of the education service and of our hopes for its further development.

Since that first Exeter conference we have, for better or worse, witnessed the gradual 'demythologizing' of primary education (Richards, 1980). HMI surveys, in particular, have helped to strip primary and middle schools of many myths, both positive and negative. The 'quickening trend' towards enquiry-based approaches detected by Plowden has not materialized on a substantial scale in top infant, junior or middle school classes; 'the primary school revolution' appears not to have been tried and found wanting but never to have been tried at all except in a small number of schools; most

Source: First published in Galton, M. and Moon, B. (eds.) (1983) *Changing Schools, Changing Curriculum* Harper & Row, London.

teachers have not responded in the 'open', 'flexible', 'experimental' way curriculum developers fondly assumed they would. In retrospect, most proposals for curriculum change made in the 1960s and early 1970s were based on assumptions of teaching and learning which were not shared by the majority of teachers. At present, the curriculum in most schools appears to be a revamped version of the elementary school curriculum—revamped to include some new elements, especially but not only in mathematics, but retaining the same major utilitarian emphases as its predecessor. To describe it so is not necessarily to condemn it. In some classes, the traditional elementary curriculum remains virtually unscathed: reading, writing and ciphering predominate. In a small number of schools, very substantial curriculum changes have presumably taken place, though the experience of such schools has not been documented by those of us interested in curriculum research and development. Judging from the evidence, the major distinguishing feature of primary education during the last twenty years has been organizational rather than curricular change—in particular, the remarkable spread of non-streaming, the introduction of vertical grouping in a substantial number of infant and junior schools, and the resultant changes in internal class organization including a much larger degree of individualization of work. This picture may not be very comforting to those who have worked hard to transform the primary curriculum or still cherish the possibility of its wholesale transformation, but does represent the general situation which curriculum development agencies and agents have to address during the next decade.

This exploration of the next decade is in three parts:

(a) a brief examination of certain logistical features which are likely to affect the response that teachers in primary and middle schools make to curriculum issues;

(b) a review of major curriculum issues likely to be 'in currency' in the 1980s;

(c) a brief discussion of the possible impact of these issues on primary education in the light of the features discussed in (a) and the receptivity of schools to change, as revealed by surveys and researches.

LOGISTICAL FEATURES

Firstly, the next decade will see the continuance of primary and middle schools as institutions recognizably similar to those which exist at present. This is not as trite a comment as it appears at first sight. Middle schools are under attack from a variety of quarters in the light of falling rolls, sixth-form reorganization and uncertainty as to their effectiveness (Taylor and Garson, 1982). Middle schools, however, will still be with us in 1992, not in every local education authority which currently has them but in sufficient numbers to constitute a small but significant minority of schools, catering for children in the middle years. The primary school, too, is likely to come under attack towards the end of the decade by those who will argue that it is an anachronistic institution in the age of the computer-based information revolution. However, Papert's (1980) dream of educationally powerful computational environments where learning takes place with LOGO but without a curriculum is unlikely to be realized on a large scale by 1992, nor Stonier's society where most of children's education is via the television screen in their own homes and where primary teachers are replaced by surrogate grandparents (1982). For the next decade at least, the primary school is likely to be more secure as an institution than its secondary counterpart whose existence in its present form seems increasingly threatened by falling rolls (which will continue into the 1990s), the inroads of the Manpower Services Commission, the reorganization of 16–19 provision and the indifference or even hostility of many of its clients. By 1992 we could be much nearer a scenario where primary education from 4 to 14 is the only institutional and compulsory form of schooling, following on from which there is a variety of educational provision on offer with appropriately supported opportunities for would-be students to re-enter the educational system later in their lives, if they so wish.

A second logistical feature is the fall and possible rise of pupil numbers through the 1980s. The primary school population in England and Wales reached a peak in 1973 when there were about five and a quarter million children in maintained nursery and primary schools; by 1979 numbers had fallen by about half a million and by 1980 will have fallen by about a further million (Collings, 1980). This steep decline presages further school closures and amalgamations, more staff redeployment, smaller schools and more mixed-age classes, and threatens the preservation of the existing curriculum in many primary and middle schools as staff leave or, more likely, retire and are not replaced. But after 1986, what? Certainly a slight rise for a while, but for how long and at what rate? Will the rise be the first step out of the trough of pupil numbers, will it soon level out, or will it be merely a hiccup in a downward trend which will continue into the 1990s? (For one view see Dennison, 1981; for another see DES, 1982.)

If map projections distort, then population projections distract. They distract us from coming to terms with the period we are now experiencing and will experience till at least 1986. They encourage us to believe that the present situation is temporary, to be endured rather than entered into enthusiastically; with problems which need only be tackled in a makeshift fashion, making the best of a bad job until better times come along; with hopes and ambitions deferred rather than sought or modified in the light of current circumstances. Population projections which are inevitably going to be wrong to some degree are too slender supports to be relied on for the purpose of sustaining developments in primary education or planning personal careers. The possibility has to be faced that pupil numbers may not rise for more than a few years after 1986, or, if they do rise, may rise very slowly and then in a climate unlikely to be characterized by the heady expansionism of the late 1950s and 1960s. Whether we are considering curriculum development or our own careers, we would be wise not to depend too much on a late 1980s equivalent of the 'golden age' of twenty years before.

A third logistical feature which will affect developments is the level of financial support given to the education service, a factor dependent on the state of the economy, the role within it of public expenditure, and the relative importance accorded educational expenditure compared with other forms of public expenditure. Educational expenditure reached a peak in the middle of the last decade and has faltered somewhat since then. To use MacDonald's apt analogy, big spending services such as education 'ground to a crawl as the hare of public expenditure was harnessed to the tortoise of economic growth' (1979, p. 28). What about the next decade? At what rate will the crawl proceed? The cynics may ask in what direction? The education lobby has to cope not only with a decline in pupil numbers but also with the effects of an ageing population which means that the claims of rival competitors, especially social services, may prove much more persuasive. The situation might be different with a different political administration but probably only marginally so. In the spring of 1982 the White Paper *The Government's Expenditure Plans 1982-3 to 1984-5* was published. During that period, government's expenditure on education is due to increase by eight percent in monetary terms, but this does not allow for the rate of inflation. Assuming an average inflation rate of 6 percent per year (an optimistic forecast judging from the recent past) overall prices would increase by about 18 percent during the period. In consequence, on this prediction, real spending on education would fall by about 10 percent up to 1984–1985. Based on the figures given in the White Paper, Peston argues that education's share of public expenditure which has fallen steadily since 1977 would stand at 10.4 percent during 1984–1985; his calculations suggest that 'this will take education back to a position similar to what it was in the late 1950s or early 1960s' (p. 2). Of course, government expenditure on schools might increase in the latter half of the decade, but by how much and at what rate? It seems almost certain that primary education will operate against a background of continued, if occasionally mitigated, financial constraint, but this does not rule out all developments. After all, during the late 1950s and early 1960s much expenditure was devoted to providing 'roofs over heads', a problem which is unlikely to be particularly pressing during the late 1980s. It should be possible to provide some expenditure for developing or strengthening the primary/middle school curriculum.

Other probable background features to the next decade could have been sketched out. The three featured here have been included to provide some kind of backcloth against which likely issues for the primary curriculum can be discussed. The future is unlikely to be as expansive as we would like nor as retrospective as we fear. It will be a period of restraint, but restraint does not automatically bring with it stagnation or regression. To return to Mac-Donald's analogy, the hare and the tortoise do not have to remain stationary, nor necessarily need they turn tail and retreat.

CURRICULUM ISSUES

Against this backcloth, what curriculum issues will be raised? What pressures will be placed on primary and middle schools? What topics will feature in in-service courses and in future conferences?

Most fundamentally, primary and middle schools will be under increasing pressure from the DES, from HMI and from local education authorities (though not, perhaps, from most parents) to devise intellectually challenging curricula, widely defined and adequately justified. The emphasis on intellectual development, powerfully represented in the primary survey and in the section on the primary phase in *The School Curriculum 1981*, is likely to intensify. It will involve the re-examination of assumptions about what young children can and cannot learn, it will require consideration of the skills, ideas, rules and generalizations underlying areas of understanding, and it will lead to the advocacy of curricula which clearly embody such skills and ideas. It is likely to lead to pressures for the extension of carefully planned programmes of work to areas beyond the basics for younger as well as older children. Support for such a position is provided by White in the final chapter of *The Aims of Education Restated* (1982): 'Children's minds do not develop naturally and in due season like biological entities; conceptual schemes are acquired only in social interaction and can be extended by deliberate intervention. . . . Understanding is a matter of degree, not an all-or-nothing affair. Children of eight or nine may not be capable of a very profound understanding of such concepts as democracy, or the trade balance, or electricity, but there is no reason why they should not have *some* grasp of these things, as well as some purchase on recent world history and current affairs and some capacity to enjoy music, poetry and the other arts' (pp. 157, 158). As White implies, this emphasis on intellectual development need not be at the expense of the arts (though financial restrictions may put these under increasing strain unless they are protected); it may even add an appreciative dimension to the performance aspect of the arts which is at present dominant in schools. A more challenging curriculum requires deepened understanding of subject matter and of children's learning, greater intraprofessional collaboration and sharing of expertise, and more clearly articulate co-ordination of the efforts of individual schools and teachers. Increasingly, policies will be required to co-ordinate and reinforce the impact of individual initiatives taken by practitioners within schools and to co-ordinate the work of individual schools within local authorities (Richards, 1982).

As part of this intellectual emphasis, schools will be required to refine the nature of 'basic' skills beyond decoding, ciphering and writing for a teacher-audience, so as to include a range of higher-level skills previously considered by many as appropriate for only a small minority of children. The primary survey has already set this in train. Basic to most children's education up to thirteen will be skills involved, for example, in following and presenting arguments, in evaluating various kinds of evidence, in speculating about motives, in approaching the printed word in different ways for different purposes, in writing for a variety of audiences, in setting up different kinds of inquiry and in classifying and generalizing in relation to phenomena encountered in a variety of curriculum areas. It is not, of course, the case that these skills have never before been taught in primary or middle schools; some schools have long redefined what they considered to be basic to a child's education. What is new is the requirement, as outlined in *The School Curriculum,* for all schools to redefine the basics (and incidentally, to re-educate governors and parents to accept, and to demand, the resources to implement the redefinition). It needs to be emphasized how strong the challenge will be to the long-accepted basis of primary education: the 'basic basics', as one observer calls them, are firmly embedded in our assumptions as well as our practices.

Three areas of the curriculum, in particular, are likely to be the focus of considerable activity during the next few years. The impetus to developing primary science will almost certainly continue. The inclusion of primary science in the government's statement of guidance on the school curriculum, the advocacy of HMI, the efforts of LEAs in producing guidelines and providing Inset, and the proliferation of published schemes with, at long last, accompanying pupils' materials, will see to that. Getting science of any kind going will be a priority in many primary schools; in others and in middle schools, where science is much more firmly established, more attention will be given to how teacher-directed practical work can be complemented by more open-ended activities where children frame questions based on their own observations, suggest patterns in what is observed, offer explanations of what has caused the patterns and test their suggested explanations. Greater use of the local environment for ecological investigations is likely to be stressed as in the application of science to other areas of the curriculum and the use of mathematics to help children express scientific ideas and relationships.

Craft, design and technology are second areas likely to be increasingly advanced as candidates for development at top primary and middle school levels. At present, in most schools, little demanding work is done in relation to craft, or to design or to technology. The absence of the latter in schools is neatly highlighted in this quotation from Evans, an advocate of primary technology: 'Of nuts and bolts and metal and wires used to conduct electricity, of practical reasoning, of the use of powerful imagination—as distinct from the pixilated stuff of creative writing—and of the application of science and mathematics in the design of working gadgets, there is rarely a sign' (1980, p. 21). Craft, design and technology are intended to give boys and girls skills in the identification and solution of practical problems, including the design and construction of devices which perform practical functions. In tackling such problems, children are introduced to the physical and aesthetic properties of materials such as wood, metal and plastics, and are involved in a variety of processes—defining problems, considering possible solutions, selecting, designing, constructing, operating, appraising, modifying, using, etc. The moves towards establishing craft, design and technology as a central concern of the middle-year curriculum are in their infancy; the next few years should see clearer expectations established as to the skills and capacities to be developed, the range of activities to be included in programmes of work and the material provision required to sustain this work. CDT is likely to be demanding of resources, and there is a danger that its development might be at the expense of the other arts; if so, an important and, in some schools, distinguished area of the curriculum might be put at risk.

Mathematics post-Cockcroft is an obvious focus of attention, though less so than science or CDT. This is partly because primary mathematics received a moderately good press in Cockcroft: 'There has been a general widening of the mathematics curriculum in most primary schools during the last twenty years to include both a greater understanding of number and also work on measurement, shape and space, graphical representation and the development of simple logical ideas. We believe that this broadening of the curriculum has had a beneficial effect both in improving children's attitudes towards mathematics and also in laying the foundations of better understanding' (1982, paragraph 296). Future activity is likely to be focused on the use of calculators and, to a lesser extent, microcomputers, as teaching and learning aids, on the extension and refinement of mathematical language through more extended and considered use of class and small-group discussion, on the application of mathematics to everyday problems and to other areas of the curriculum, and on the planning and co-ordination of mathematics throughout primary and middle schools. Hopefully also, researchers including teacher-researchers may take up Cockcroft's suggestions for studies into the language of mathematics texts, tests and lessons, into children's spontaneous problem-solving activities and into the extent to which strategies and processes for problem solving can be taught.

In addition to curriculum development in science, CDT and mathematics, there will be renewed attempts to introduce three curricular dimensions to inform the planning of the work in different subjects and to provide means of inter-relating such work. The first of these, multicultural education, draws on the experiences of the cultures that make up contemporary British society in order to help children understand the nature of the society and to provide them with a basis for understanding how our society is similar to, and different from, other societies. To achieve this, a multicultural perspective will have to permeate work across the curriculum in all schools, irrespective of whether they have pupils from ethnic minority groups. The second dimension is environmental education, a concept broader than environmental studies, which seeks to develop children's understanding of, and concern for, their own environment and that of others and to help them participate in making informed decisions about environmental issues. Education 'for', 'from' and 'about' the environment are its catchwords; all three aspects will be stressed in the ecologically conscious 1980s. The last dimension is health education, already the subject of considerable curriculum development activity but not yet adequately embodied in curricula. As curricular dimensions rather than timetabled subjects, all three are likely to be overlooked in practice unless there is careful planning and co-ordination at school level. Increasingly, schools will be asked to indicate in what ways their curricula contribute to these three broad areas.

The use of microcomputers is inevitably going to be an important issue for the next decade, not because primary or middle school teachers want it to be but because government, manufacturers and public opinion will make it so. The major question is not whether something called computer studies or the like should be a new area of the curriculum but how far micros can be used to help us in the difficult task of creating that intellectually challenging curriculum described earlier. Micros in primary schools are still news, with all the dangers that newsworthiness brings. In the *Times Educational Supplement* of 19 March 1982, Spencer reported the government's plans to help primary schools buy their own microcomputers as part of a £1000 million boost for new technology announced in that year's budget. The MEP (Microelectronics in Education Programme) is also issuing software for use in primary schools.

In line with my other rather conservative predictions, I do not believe that micros are going to transform schooling in general or primary and middle schools in particular over the next decade. As Cockcroft aptly and comfortingly points out, 'we are still at a very early stage in the development of their use as an aid to teaching mathematics. The amount of work which needs to be done before microcomputers are likely to have any major effect on mathematics teaching is very great indeed' (1982, paragraph 403). If that is an accurate reflection of the situation as regards mathematics, then an enormous amount of work has to be done in relation to other areas of the curriculum. At present and in the immediate future, the most important concerns are not to get micros into every primary school but the production of good quality software and the encouragement of careful and *documented* experimentation in a relatively small number of schools (not all of which should be staffed by enthusiasts), on the basis of which local education authorities can devise and implement policies for the gradual introduction and realistic application of micros across the curriculum, not just in mathematics. Such small-scale work should focus particularly on the devising of conceptually based programs which invite children to tease out possibilities in the situations presented, to speculate about explanations and consequences, to derive generalizations and to formulate and test their hypotheses. Parallel with experimentation in the teaching situation, computer literacy courses for the rest of us in primary education need to be mounted to help us understand the nature of the new technology and to expand our awareness of its potential in the long term and its likely impact on practice in the short term. Micros promise to be an important tool in providing an intellectually challenging curriculum, provided the drill and practice programs common at present are complemented by simulations, by information retrieval and processing and by opportunities for some children, at least, to devise their own programs (see Garland, 1982).

This account of curriculum issues likely to be 'in currency' in the 1980s concludes by brief reference to the general issues of continuity and consistency which have underpinned much discussion of the school curriculum since the mid-1970s. Continuity is concerned with the degree to which curricular activities offered children relate to, and build on, their previous experience. Four forms can be distinguished: (a) the continuity which children experience between learning in the home and learning at school, not just at entry age but throughout the primary/middle school phase, (b) the continuity children experience in any one class in the course of a school year, (c) the continuity they experience as they move from class to class within the same school, and (d) the continuity they experience as they move from one stage of schooling to the next. Up to now most progress has been made in relation to (b), most professional discussion has focused on (d), but as the 1980s proceed, more attention is likely to be paid to (c) through closer co-ordination of programmes of work within schools, and, possibly, towards the end of the decade to (a) as more children have access to data bases through their television sets and personal computers, as more parents have the time and confidence consciously to teach their children the skills and knowledge they value and as the concept of school, particularly at the secondary stage, is called into question by a vociferous minority of parents.

The last six or seven years have seen growing pressures for greater consistency and coherence in the education offered children. Since 1976 the DES has expressed its public concern at the diversity of practice that has emerged at secondary and primary levels. A string of publications from *Educating Our Children* (1977) to *The School Curriculum* (1981) bear witness to this concern. In the primary context, the issue was highlighted by chapter six of the primary survey which reported very considerable inconsistencies in the curricular activities offered by primary classes and argued that 'ways of providing a more consistent coverage for important aspects of the curriculum need to be examined' (1978, paragraph 6.9). It would appear that developments towards creating more consistent curricula are taking place at three levels. Through *The School Curriculum* (1981) and a number of follow-up documents the DES is attempting to set out a broad structure for the curriculum at a national level; through the issuing of curriculum guidelines (and the closer monitoring of the work of schools through inspection, testing or other forms of data-gathering) local education authorities are responding to DES initiatives and in the process are devising broad curriculum policies for their schools; through self-evaluation procedures, curriculum reviews and the strengthening of the position of post-holders, schools are being urged to appraise their curricula and to modify these in the light of guidance, whether from LEA guidelines, from evaluation panels or from individual inspectors or advisers. These moves towards greater consistency are not likely to result, by 1992, in the detailed control of the school curriculum by central government, but could result in the removal of some of the more extreme curricular inequalities among schools and could help provide a more consistent set of experiences for more pupils for a greater part of their time in school, which I believe, is necessary if a more genuinely comprehensive education is to be provided in the primary/middle school phase (Richards, 1982).

ISSUES AND ACTUALITIES

A number of pressures for change in the 1980s have been outlined, but what of actualities? How far will such pressures be realized in the light of the backcloth described earlier and of schools' proven capacity to absorb and neutralize curriculum innovation?

Generalizing about schools is difficult enough; the difficulty is compounded when generalization is to be accompanied by prediction. Between now and 1992 there will be a considerable number of schools which will provide the kind of challenging curriculum outlined in this paper; there will be a few who will go well beyond this to offer a kind of curriculum of which this author cannot conceive. In contrast, there will be schools which will continue to prepare children very adequately for the 1980s and 1990s—as they did for the 1880s and 1890s. But what of the majority of schools?

Two scenarios are offered here. In the first, pupil numbers continue to fall, albeit with a hiccup in the mid-1980s, schools become considerably smaller, staffs become stagnant except for redeployment, local education authorities become increasingly inbred, in-service education is cut back, and isolationism at the class, school and LEA level increases. Only a token response is offered to the issues outlined, and there is an emphasis on the 'basic basics'. In the second scenario, there is some easing of demographic contraction and of financial constraint, greater mobility of staff, more co-operation among schools to share expertise and resources, better co-ordination of curricula among schools in a locality, greater availability of in-service education and a moderate influx of newly qualified teachers, some of whom are particularly knowledgeable in mathematics, science or craft, design and technology. Overall, a genuine attempt is made to respond to the curriculum issues discussed above.

Perhaps the next few years will see a continuing shift towards the realization of the first scenario. Perhaps the latter half of the decade will see developments leading to the realization of the second.

REFERENCES

Bennett, N. *et al.* (1980) *Open Plan Schools*, NFRH.

Collings, H. (1980) Falling rolls, in Richards, E. (ed.), *Primary Education for the Eighties*, A. & C. Black.

DENI (1981) *Primary Education: report of an inspectorate survey in Northern Ireland*, HMSO.

Dennison, W. (1981) *Education in Jeopardy: problems and possibilities of contraction*, Basil Blackwell.

DES (1977) *Educating Our Children*, HMSO.

DES Welsh Office (1981) *The School Curriculum.*

DES (1978) *Primary Education in England: a survey by HM Inspectors of Schools*, HMSO.

DES (1982) *Pupils and School Leavers: future numbers*, Report on Education No. 97, HMSO.

Evans, P. (1980) Science: pure or applied? *Education 3–13*, 8:1, pp. 16–23.

Galton, M., Simon, B. and Croll, P. (1980) *Inside the Primary Classroom*, Routledge & Kegan Paul.

Garland, R. (ed.) (1982) *Computers and Children in the Primary School*, The Falmer Press.

MacDonald, B. (1979) Hard times: educational accountability in England, *Educational Analysis*, Vol. 1, pp. 23–43.

Papert, S. (1980) *Mindstorms: children, computers and powerful ideas*, Harvester Press.

Peston, M. (1982) Sir Geoffrey's framework for decline, *Times Educational Supplement*, 12 March.

Richards, C. (1980) Demythologizing primary education, *Journal of Curriculum Studies*, 12, pp. 77.

Richards, C. (ed.) (1982) *New Directions in Primary Education*, The Falmer Press.

SED (1980) *Learning and Teaching in Primary 4 and Primary 7: a report by HM Inspectors of Schools in Scotland*, HMSO.

Spencer, D. (1982) Computers soon for primaries, *Times Educational Supplement*, 19 March.

Steadman, S. *et al.* (1979) *Impact and Take up Project: a first interim report*, Schools Council Publications.

Stonier, T. (1982) Changes in Western society: educational implications, in Richards, C. (ed.) *New Directions in Primary Education*, The Falmer Press.

Taylor, M. and Garson, Y. (1982) *Schooling in the Middle Years*, Trentham Books.

The Government's Expenditure plans 1982–3 to 1984–5 (1982) Cmnd 8494–1, HMSO.

White, J. (1982) *The Aims of Education Restated*, Routledge & Kegan Paul.

4

Local Education Authorities and the Curriculum

MARTEN SHIPMAN

Discussion about recent changes in the location of control over the school curriculum in England and Wales has usually been confined to central government and the teachers. This not only neglects the third partner, the Local Education Authorities (LEAs), but ignores their legal responsibilities. The 1944 Education Act gave them a statutory duty to contribute to the spiritual, moral and physical development of the communities they serve. In law, the curriculum in all bar voluntary aided schools is the responsibility of the LEA. This responsibility is usually delegated to governing bodies of schools. But LEAs not only provide the buildings and the resources for schools, recruit and pay the teachers, but must ensure that ' . . . efficient education . . . shall be available to meet the needs of the population of their area' (Education Act, 1944).

Most writers looking at the education service in England conclude that it is 'Pluralistic, incremental, unsystematic, reactive' (Kogan and Packwood, 1974). This untidiness leaves room for LEA initiatives. They do not merely respond to changes in their environments, whether those changes are at national or local level, or in their schools and colleges. They also initiate developments that affect the remaining partners of the service. This is the model used in this chapter. LEAs are seen as interacting, creating pressure on central government, on schools and colleges, parents and pressure groups, as well as responding to stresses built up as changes occur in other parts of the service (see, for example, Howell and Brown, 1983). This is a systems model, capable of suggesting explanations about the way the service is maintained in a stable condition, but less satisfactory for examining the impact of sustained financial constraint from central government, or of radical changes in the

Specially commissioned for this volume © The Open University Press, 1985.

distribution of power between the different parties involved. Here a model showing how the location of power is affected by the resources available to these parties has proved to be more illuminating (see, for example, Ranson, 1980). But even that resource-dependency model may fail to illuminate the underlying relationship between education, economy and state (Salter and Tapper, 1981). There are many theoretical models available, but they remain sources of hypotheses that often provide conflicting explanations.

In practice, the untidiness of the education service defeats attempts to use a single, simple model as a source of understanding. This is particularly the case in examining the curriculum, where influence is distributed between central and local government, teachers, lecturers and many pressure groups. It is clear that sustained financial contraction has shifted power towards central government, just as expansion in the 1960s increased the freedom and capacity of teachers to take initiatives in their schools and colleges. But even that generalization obscures the variety among LEAs and their response to changing times. It is possible to place LEA curriculum policies along a spectrum from *responsive* or *reactive* to *initiatory* or *proactive*. Second, pressures on LEAs arrive above, from central government, national committees, research and development reports and HMI, or below from teachers in the 30,000 institutions, or from the manifold interest groups in the locality. Whether top-down, bottom-up or lateral, these pressures can be met by passive or active policies. Third, responses cannot be limited to the radical or progressive. LEAs are ranged along the whole political spectrum from extreme Left to extreme Right, and a traditional, back-to-basics response is as much a policy as a drive for greater equality or opportunity through positive discrimination.

LEAs have to be involved with the curriculum because they are not only legally responsible, but are legally bound to serve their communities, and these communities take a close interest in the content of the schooling of children. Across the 1960s a watchful stance seemed sufficient in county or town hall. The curriculum was left to the teachers under the largely nominal role of governing bodies who acted for the LEA. The dismissal of the teachers from the William Tyndale School following their attempt to introduce a radical curriculum is a watershed because of the Auld Report (1976) on this case, which re-asserted that the LEA retained legal responsibility for the curriculum and criticized the failure to exercise it. But it would be misleading to see the William Tyndale case as more than the tip of an iceberg of corrective measures in all county and town halls which have always acted to limit excessive diversity. The daily discussions, visits, inspections, circulars, in-service courses and committees involving heads, teachers, advisers, inspectors, officers, members and governors serve as ongoing influences. All help to feed views on the curriculum to and from the schools.

THE NEGLECT OF THE LEas IN THE CURRICULUM DEBATE

The reasons for the neglect of the LEAs in the debate over the control of the curriculum in the late 1970s are important for the light they throw on LEA responsibilities. First, across the 1960s and 1970s, the burgeoning academic literature was primarily concerned with curriculum changes. The focus of work on curriculum theory and evaluation was on the novel and the marginal. LEAs, with years of investment in buildings, resources and teachers had to be concerned with the mainstream not the latest tributary. Only when central government began to concern itself with the school curriculum in the late 1970s did academic attention switch from projects to the main body of subjects that were the continuing concern of the LEAs.

The second reason for the neglect of LEAs was a confusion in academic thinking about the foreground and background factors influencing the curriculum. Births had started to fall in 1965 and intakes to the infant schools from 1970. This was exacerbated by migration from the inner cities. By the early 1970s LEAs were starting to plan for shrinking primary schools. Simultaneously, there was concern over the increase in public expenditure which had risen from 42 to 50 per cent of gross national product across the 1960s. Both Labour and Conservative administrations were worried. The Treasury committee under Lord Plowden recommended ways of aligning government spending to the state of the economy in 1961. By the mid-1960s central and local government was subject to planning that was to lead, year after year, to the increasingly tighter controls now imposed, particularly cash limits on expenditure. At the same time the political consensus broke. This applied locally as well as nationally as parents used the courts to oppose the ending of secondary selection. The LEAs were under increasing demographic, financial and political constraints through the 1970s. As early as 1970 an LEA officer could state that 'the education officer is a prisoner not the architect of the system' (Birley, 1970). The constraining factors were the foreground for the LEAs in planning the curriculum of schools and colleges, yet academics still concentrated on the Schools Council and on models of development that bore little relation to the harsh reality on the ground.

The third reason for the common misunderstanding of the role of LEAs is the academic tendency to extract features of practice and policy as if they were isolated. School and curriculum self-evaluation is a typical example, treated as if it were not part of the total arrangements for monitoring in an authority and, as a consequence, often misunderstood (Shipman, 1982). Anyone, for example, who believed that the Inner London Education Authority relied solely on responses to the self-evaluation questions to check the content of the curriculum and the standards achieved in schools was ignoring the sophisticated and extensive programme of evaluation of which this document formed a small part. It is important to remember that LEAs develop policies incrementally. Each new development, whether a set of guidelines, a new test programme or an in-service course will be added to the capital stock of related measures built up through years of investment. Furthermore, it is only within this established framework that new developments can be interpreted.

The final factor accounting for the underestimation of the LEA role in developing and implementing curriculum policies was the tendency to see the many ways in which influence was brought to bear as specific, uni-purpose techniques. In practice, curriculum guidelines, checkpoints, transfer documents, profiles, tests, self-evaluation booklets, inspections, in-service courses and so on serve many different purposes. Every teacher appreciates this. Being asked to attend a course is more than a request to learn about some new aspect of the curriculum. It is liable to include being evaluated by the inspectors organizing it, being considered for promotion, being sounded out about possible new developments and being asked to express views on existing practices. An example comes in the account of the expansion of standardized testing in LEAs at the start of the 1980s (Gipps *et al.*, 1983). Three Conservative authorities are stated to be using tests for monitoring standards. But the act of monitoring also lays down definitions of what is expected to be taught, at which age and in what sequence. In one of the Labour authorities testing is said to be for 'professional' purposes, to identify children requiring help over reading. But the headteachers in this study saw that testing is an emphatic way of defining the importance of reading. This was not lost on critics of the Assessment of Performance Unit (Gipps and Goldstein, 1983). Similarly the vogue for self-evaluation questions distributed to schools by LEAs in the early 1980s was not just a way of ensuring thought about the curriculum. It was a way of defining a model for it. When an LEA asks 'Has the school programmes of work or guidelines in all or any of the following areas of the curriculum: physical education? language and literacy?' etc. (Inner London Education Authority, 1977), the hidden agenda reads that there should be such programmes or guidelines.

When these four factors are taken into account the potential of an LEA to take initiatives as well as to respond to various pressures becomes more apparent. We have a system that is national but locally administered. Responsibilities have to be fulfilled with limited resources. With over twenty years of attempts to restrain public expenditure by the Treasury, the allocation to local authorities, within them to the education service, within the service to the various sectors, between and within schools and colleges, had become intensely political. LEAs were under increased pressure from local interest groups, teachers and lecturers long before Prime Minister Callaghan's Ruskin College speech in 1976 which initiated the Great Debate on education. There was no prospect of LEAs being able to buy a way through the problems faced. How then did LEAs respond to demands made on them and sustain initiatives?

LOCAL RESPONSES TO NATIONAL PRESSURES

The 1944 Act gave the Minister of Education ultimate responsibility for the maintenance of standards of education. It empowered him to intervene if an LEA, or the governing body of a maintained school acted unreasonably in using a statutory power or in discharging a duty. This power has rarely been used, but defines where the limits of partnership lie. In practice there is a stream of Statutory Instruments, Administrative Memoranda and letters giving information, laying down procedures and regulations, and signposting changes in educational policy. The service works through these administrative controls and the Education Acts have tended to substitute them for legal rules. This enables regulations to be updated without going through Parliament. The Acts have been very generally worded thus allowing the maximum flexibility in interpretation and implementation (Mann, 1979).

In the late 1970s central government began to take a close interest in the school curriculum. This took the form of increased activity by Her Majesty's Inspectors (HMI), publications on the content of the school curriculum (DES, 1980 and 1981) and the issuing of Circular 14/77 inviting LEAs to review and report on their policies and practices in relation to the school curriculum. The DES was asking LEAs for an account of their responsibility for the curriculum which many had left to the teachers over the previous decade. This reminder was seen as a threat by the organized teachers who had assumed their right to act autonomously. The National Union of Teachers opposed the move as 'interventionist' (Doe, 1978). When the report of the survey was published it was clear that many LEAs had not seen that they had an active role to play (DES, 1979). It was made clear that the DES intended following up the exercise to make sure they did. The DES view was unambiguous. 'To fulfil their responsibilities effectively within any nationally agreed framework authorities must exercise leadership and interpret national policies and objectives in the light of local needs and circumstances' (DES, 1979, p. 3). There was to be a national framework and LEAs were to lead the teachers, not respond to local changes.

Such direct interventions by central government are rare. More common is involvement in developments throughout the service that are finally made a national issue through committee reports, curriculum projections or administrative action by central government. The three examples that follow are all concerned with trends that steadily increased the pressure for adaptation at local level. But it has to be remembered that many of these trends reached the national level of a committee such as Plowden, or Bullock or Warnock, or a Schools Council Project, or a decision to stop elevating the status of Further Education Colleges to Polytechnics, after much activity within LEAs. The examples are concerned with events as much initiated by LEAs as presented to them for response from above.

The publication of an important report on education is usually followed by

LEA initiatives to ensure that there is a response from the schools. But it has to be remembered that Bullock on language, or Cockcroft on mathematics would be preceded by local developments. LEAs respond, but they, and their teachers, have always played a part in setting the context for the report and provided many of the examples of good practice. When *A Language for Life* (Bullock, 1975) was published, many LEAs, particularly in the inner cities, were already concerned with standards of literacy, had organized test programmes and in-service courses, and increased the advisory service in this specialized area. The response of the Inner London Education Authority (ILEA) to publication was typical. Multiple copies were bought and circulated. The Inspectorate prepared a summary, repeated the main recommendations and asked for a response from all schools. The report was discussed at three consultative committees involving teachers, at meetings of members, inspectors and officers, and between HMI who had helped produce the report and ILEA inspectors. An action research project was launched in selected schools. All were asked to prepare a programme of language across the curriculum. Series of teacher-centre and school-based in-service courses were organized. As responses came back to county hall, inspectors produced further papers and organized more local conferences. This activity was reported back to members on Schools Sub-Committee. In time the action became part of normal routine. The evidence and the recommendations in the report had exerted influence in the context of ongoing LEA action.

A similar process was observed in research on the Keele Integrated Studies Project as it was trialled in four Midland LEAs in the early 1970s (Shipman, Bolam and Jenkins, 1974). The project team introduced its version of integrated studies with the cachet of the Schools Council. The LEA advisers were supportive, but had already been tentatively promoting versions of integration that did not coincide with that of the project. They protected these versions to the point of seeming to undermine the Schools Council project. This was cocooned within the framework of LEA policy and practice. Local advisers justified this apparently subversive action through reference to the limited life of the project compared with their own continuing responsibilities for the curriculum which had the support of the authority.

It should also be noted that this was before the Great Debate and in the era of apparent teacher autonomy. Yet LEAs saw the curriculum as their ultimate responsibility when faced with innovation sponsored by the Schools Council. It may have been covert, but any threats from outside to local policies were rapidly identified, insulated or transformed, until aligned to the local pattern.

The final example is the ILEAs review of its Vocational Further Education Service between 1970 and 1973, documented by Brown (in Howell and Brown, 1983), then an officer of the Authority. While this was primarily concerned with the reorganization of further education, it was also about the curriculum of schools as well as colleges. For example, the distribution of

GCE A level between FE colleges, and between them and the recently established comprehensive schools, became a major issue, particularly as the authority was already planning for secondary provision in the light of school rolls which were already falling in the primary schools and had been projected to show a large surplus of secondary school places in the 1980s.

Brown's study illustrates clearly how pressures built up to produce reorganization. In 1966 central government decided that advanced courses would be concentrated in polytechnics and that there would be only a limited number of these. Meanwhile increasing numbers were staying on at school, rather than going on to FE colleges. The ILEA's structure of senior and junior colleges was increasingly seen as inappropriate for the new situation and pressure built up for a single tier of multipurpose colleges outside the polytechnics. Brown describes how the teachers through the Association of Teachers in Technical Institutions (ATTI) and the college principals through the Association of Principals of ILEA Technical Colleges and Schools of Art (APTC) built up the pressure for change, particularly through the Standing Advisory Committee for Further Education (SACFE). This committee has teachers from the further education teacher unions and met political members, as well as sitting with ILEA officers.

Once the Review had started the momentum was sustained by ILEA officers on an FE Steering Committee, working through a special Review Working Party. Reports and the final proposals went to members on the Policy Coordinating Committee, Further and Higher Sub-Committee and hence to the Education Committee. But it is the process of mobilizing support that demonstrates the way LEAs sustain policies. The Review Working Party was a way of involving the teachers through consultation and of producing a flow of information. In the end the ILEA officers implemented proposals that were little changed across the years of the review. They had a clear picture of the FE service they wanted, and of its relation with the schools and adult institutes. The teachers and principals were influential, particularly at the start of the review. But the continuity was provided by the policy worked out by the officers of the Authority. This was a major determinant of the organization finally agreed, although teachers, members, pressure groups and the DES exerted influence on the way.

These three examples have been used to emphasize that LEAs are organised to allow for many influences, both legal and professional, that impinge upon them. But in all three the response was aligned to ongoing policies. It is easy to overlook both this complexity and consistency. The consultative committees within and the formalized links with central government, other LEAs and the teachers are only the most visible part of the total structure through which influences flow both in and out of town and county halls. But all these influences meet, or arise from, policies that have been developed incrementally over the years. They rarely exist as statements or documents, but are apparent as soon as responses are necessary to some external development such as the raising of the school-leaving age, a major national report, or an accelerating trend in schools or colleges. These policies also account for the initiatives taken locally. Once again these are not just responses to trends in local schools, or the imposition of policies from the education office. As with nationally initiated changes they arise in the political interaction that is the day-to-day business in and around county or town halls, schools and colleges, and the pressure groups which compete to obtain their own preferred distribution of scarce resources.

LEA RESPONSES TO SCHOOL-BASED INITIATIVES

LEAs exercise their responsibilities for the curriculum by responding to changes introduced by teachers as well as to national developments. Their own initiatives also have these top-down and bottom-up dimensions. The key figures in the latter are the local advisers or inspectors. They work from county or town hall, usually under a chief inspector who works closely with the chief education officer (CEO). Thus senior administrative officers in the LEA are kept informed of developments in the schools. But once again it is tempting to ignore the context within which this advice occurs. Most CEOs and assistant education officers are ex-teachers and maintain their contacts with the teachers on consultative committees and through direct contacts with schools. That enables them, with their colleagues in the advisory service, to keep members informed and to influence the direction of curriculum change.

This organization within an LEA to ensure that school-based developments are monitored has been strengthened since Circular 14/77 showed an attitude of 'leave it to the teachers' that in some cases bordered on an abdication of responsibility for the curriculum by the LEA (DES, 1979). But it remains a relaxed, professional relationship in most cases, disturbed by the lack of resources to fund new developments rather than by any rigid instruction. The extent of this relaxation and the continuing freedom available to teachers to innovate can be gauged from any comparison with other education systems where syllabus, textbooks and teaching methods can be regulated from the ministry (see, for example, Hough, 1984).

The most remarkable recent grassroots development has been the abandonment of streaming in primary schools and its diminution in the secondary sector. After publication of the Plowden Report in 1967, teachers switched to mixed ability grouping, taking advantage of the relaxation following the ending of selection for secondary schooling. This was the one major and lasting change of that period and it was initiated by teachers (Simon, 1981). Indeed, the speed with which unstreaming came often surprised LEAs, for teachers needed no permission to act on their own professional judgements. In the ILEA the rate of unstreaming in secondary schools became known through a survey of reading which included questions on class organization (ILEA, 1975). Inspectors had appreciated that the development was under way, but not the extent of the change.

The development of the progressive primary school is rightly singled out as the most striking teacher-initiated curriculum development of recent decades. Reading Coe (1974), an Oxfordshire adviser, the sense of excitement is apparent as he not only sees progressive methods spreading, but appreciates their variety. But it is again necessary to put this into context. Coe describes how he moved from trying to influence schools to adopt the pattern he was used to, to sharing ideas with the teachers but leaving them to work out their own balance of practices. The Oxfordshire study centres, the teachers centres, the in-service courses, the visits by inspectors and advisers, were the mechanisms through which the LEA influenced the teachers and school policies.

LEAs AS INITIATORS

So far the *responsive* role of LEAs has been stressed. However, in every example given, the organization of LEAs has been shown to influence developments, even where these were taking place in the 30,000 schools and colleges across the country. But LEAs also *initiate* curriculum change. Oxfordshire and the West Riding of Yorkshire for primary schooling and Leicestershire, Cambridgeshire and Coventry for secondary schooling are examples where LEAs were seen as having a distinctive style. More recently, LEAs have increased the amount of standardized testing and, as a consequence, the amount of backwash, intentional or otherwise, on the curriculum (Gipps *et al.*, 1983). There has also been a proliferation of guidelines, checklists, checkpoints, position papers and policy documents published by LEAs for their schools. Many of these concern the basic skills and may have contributed to a back-to-basics movement.

The two examples that follow should be seen as continuing efforts to influence practice from town to county hall, rather than one-off enterprises. Despite changes in political control, LEAs have sustained styles of initiative. While the examples chosen are from two LEAs, Coventry and the ILEA, which have been in the van of new developments, it has also to be remembered that other LEAs have consistently adopted more traditional views of the school curriculum and would be as ready to defend these policies if pressed.

Coventry has a distinctive style of city development that goes back to the period of rebuilding following the blitz in the second world war. It pioneered comprehensive secondary schooling, then community development programmes based on schools and more recently, work experience schemes. Behind all these developments is a consistent set of principles, repeated in planning proposals over forty years. Developments are related to social and economic changes, with education seen as playing a central part in enriching the cultural life of the community. The authority is seen as having a duty to ensure that all have a chance of a dignified life. It is an active, interventionist, often controversial style justified by reference to principles of human justice.

At the end of the 1960s the city began to attract Urban Programme funds for community projects. Many of these involved the education service, particularly in providing support for teachers to work in the community and to bring that community into the schools. Educational visitors, liaison teachers, mother and toddler groups, home tuition, training programmes for parents, preventative social work based in primary schools are examples (see Coventry Education Committee, 1977). The authority established community colleges in the early 1970s and in 1983 recommended that all 11–18 secondary schools became such bases for local action (Coventry Education Committee, 1983). These developments have been organized in the 1970s by Aitken as CEO, Sanday as Chief Inspector with a particular interest in the relation of schools and industrial society, and Rennie, now Director of the Community Education Development Centre, a national body based in the town.

The publication of *Comprehensive Education for Life* (Coventry Education Committee, 1983) illustrates the incremental structure of LEA policy-making. In the first years of the 1970s, working parties were considering youth and community schemes and were to recommend the community colleges. Another working party reported in 1976 (Coventry Education Committee, 1976) on the educational needs of the 14–19 group. This stressed the central role of personal development and careers education. In 1981 *The Education of 11 to 19 year olds* was published (Coventry Education Committee, 1981) relating schooling to the changing economic circumstances in the town and asking for discussions to plan secondary education into the twenty-first century. In the same year a proposal was published that schools should become pastoral bases for all students up to 18 and that adults from all occupations should be involved in this support. The most recent proposals (Coventry Education Committee, 1983) for a common core curriculum between 11 and 13, followed by modular courses from 14 to 18, retains the emphasis of earlier proposals, particularly on personal values and universal practical experience.

The ILEA is inevitably in the public eye as the metropolitan authority and because of the size of its budget which is approaching a billion pounds. It has led the way in developing policies of positive discrimination, both in the way resources are allocated to schools and in publicizing the low attainment of identifiable groups of children (see for example ILEA, 1983). In 1981 the members elected set themselves four objectives, to improve the level of provision; to reconsider the education of the 16 to 19 group; to expand facilities for unemployed school leavers; and to examine achievement among black children, girls and working class children. This last objective was translated into policy and delivered as a series of policy documents and statements in 1983.

This drive to eliminate racism, sexism and class discrimination from the education service followed a style similar to previous developments, including the *Further Education Review* reported earlier. First, it was preceded by the collection of data and by research. Representatives of all ILEA schools were given a paper prepared by the Research and Statistics Department in September 1981. Two conferences on multi-ethnic education and the education of girls followed. Research projects were organized and, in 1983, five reviews of evidence under the general title *Race, Sex and Class* were published (ILEA, 1983). On 12 July a policy statement was adopted by the Authority, printed and circulated to all schools. Guidelines to schools were sent in September 1983 calling on staff to draw up an anti-racist policy and code and submit it to county hall. ILEA inspectorate had produced a report on equal opportunities for girls and boys in 1982 (ILEA, 1982) and a pack for use in schools to monitor progress towards sex equality was published in 1984 (ILEA, 1984). A report on the monitoring of anti-sexist initiatives was published in 1983 (ILEA, 1983).

The origins of these initiatives lie clearly with the politicians elected in 1981 and most of the publications contain an introduction by the Leader of the Authority, Frances Morrell. They are aimed at liberating the talents of black and working class children and girls. Inevitably they contain the assumption that racism, sexism and class differentiation are present in schools. The policy of aiming at assimilation is rejected. Teachers were expected to scrutinize the curriculum and eliminate racist elements. This raised a storm of protest from teachers.

The National Association of Head Teachers saw it as political interference, the NAS/UWT as reverse racism (Passmore, 1983). One headmaster resigned, calling the members political zealots (Wood, 1983). This professional opposition was accurate. Such a direct initiative over the curriculum was indeed unusual in being overtly political. Yet the political members are the final authority and were acting legally, not only within the 1944 Education Act, but in complying with the 1976 Race Relations Act and with the Equal Opportunities legislation. Furthermore, many different interests including the organized teachers had been involved in discussions over the policies for many years.

These initiatives within the ILEA are unusual in being clearly political. Yet as early as 1967 the Authority started to collect evidence on reading standards and published this for different ethnic minority groups (ILEA, 1969, 1972, 1975, 1977). These literacy surveys were started under the last Conservative majority to control the Authority. Across the 1970s the ILEA produced policy statements, strengthened support services and started to involve the minority communities. In 1977 it produced a Multi-ethnic Policy Statement and agreed to monitor progress. It co-operated with academic researchers (see, for example, Giles, 1977) and ensured that schools serving the most deprived areas received the most generous resources. Above all, the ILEA publicized the issues and produced evidence on them, even at the cost of inviting criticism.

This movement towards a policy to tackle racism as well as sexism and social class inequalities involved teachers, headteachers, officers and political members in committees and in the production of policy papers. There were standing advisory committees involving teacher union representatives and officers. Consultative committees brought together headteachers and political members.

There were parallel consultative arrangements for the further and higher education sector (see Howell and Brown, 1983). By the mid-1970s parents had been linked to the committee structure and by 1980 the black community was involved. The agendas were mostly about proposals for development, informed by the inspectorate and the research and statistics group. Across the 1970s these deliberations reflected the national shift from aiming at the integration of immigrants and cultural assimilation, to emphasising the worth of all the cultures represented in inner London. Significantly, the final thrust in the 1980s was led by the politicians and was concerned, not only with policies to overcome racism and other forms of injustices to identifiable groups, but looked for causes of that injustice in the structure of schooling and in the relation between this and the society outside the schools. The policy had emerged over a decade, but the final thrust was political, not only in the major part played by often recently elected members, but in the focus on underlying structural factors and the unequal distribution of power in society.

Policies focused on ethnic, gender and social class achievement always affect the curriculum. They are concerned with the syllabus, the teaching methods, the textbooks and the hidden curriculum of rules and regulations, relationships and rights. Such policies are high risk because they are certain to antagonize as well as assuage. For example, Bradford is seen as a leading LEA in the field of race relations and multicultural education. But this has led to trouble with the teaching force and continuing demands from the mainly Muslim minority community. The Muslim Parents' Association want to establish single-sex voluntary schools. Even with the attempts of the LEA to meet demands for the withdrawal of children from physical education, swimming and religious education, the pressure will continue, whether from existing or new interest groups among minority communities. The issues have conflict built into them. For example, sex education for girls tailored to Muslim views on the appropriate curriculum can be difficult to reconcile with a policy of eliminating sexism in schools. The educational consensus over the curriculum has broken not only because of financial constraint and a polarization of the major political parties, but because the issues of race, class and gender contain contradictory elements.

POLICIES AND POLITICS IN LEAs

The picture drawn so far has shown LEAs at the centre of many national and local pressures, both professional and legal. This balance of pressures has changed dramatically over the last decade. The DES for example has exercised its legal responsibility for maintaining standards with vigour in the 1980s. Salter and Tapper (1981) see this as a deliberate attempt to fix the agenda for the debate over education. But it has to be remembered that the Board of Education rigidly controlled the secondary school curriculum until the 1920s, when public examinations secured it with equal if not direct firmness. The Board's control over elementary schooling was equally rigid and remained into the 1930s. The persistence of selective tests for secondary school entrance held the primary curriculum through the 1950s. Indeed, it can be argued that only for a brief period in the 1960s and 1970s was there any real teacher autonomy.

What is more certain is that sustained financial stringency has moved power towards the central government who supply most of the money. Fowler (1979) has shown how decision-making has been forced back from schools to county or town halls, to the DES. Each year schools have to wait for the LEA to confirm which staff will be in post as rolls fall. But this decision has to wait for the annual grant from central government to be confirmed. Many LEAs now have a curriculum staffing policy (Bell and Higham, 1984). LEAs define a basic curriculum and then staff it, thus removing much of the freedom of teachers to decide on the curriculum to be offered. Decisions made at central government level may appear to have no implications for the school curriculum, but in the staffrooms they can result in subjects being cut out of the timetable or new grouping methods having to be adopted (Shipman, 1984).

Even so, these trends to relocate power at the centre do not necessarily inhibit local curriculum policies. So far the focus has been on innovatory authorities. But LEAs that support a traditional curriculum also have policies and have majority political support for it. A chairman of an education committee such as Muffett of Hereford and Worcester may be anathema to the teachers, but may also be reflecting the views of his constituents. When Sutton was criticized by HMI in a report on its schools, it could defend the curriculum not only because it worked, but because it was what the local people wanted. The director of education's view was 'I'd rather be criticized for a narrow curriculum and well above average examination results, than the reverse, and the parents of the borough agree' (Venning, 1983). No doubt they did and LEAs are constituted to ensure that the needs of their populations are met.

The publication of HMI reports on the relation between the level of expenditure and educational standards in LEAs had tended to bring Conservative spokespersons into the public eye as they defended their policies (see, for example, Durham, 1984). Throughout this article it has been stressed that such Right-wing curriculum policies exist alongside those derived from the liberal consensus that dominated the 1960s, or of the Left. The tendency is for the conservative policies to get little publicity alongside the more dramatic, newsworthy, radical policies. That is largely because innovation is news and interesting to both media and academia. The conservative view is that the onus for change lies with the innovator. Defending the traditional or pressing for a return to basics lacks excitement. Traditional subjects and teaching methods, subject departments and public examinations do not need overt support. Yet even an extreme radical had to admit that in popular appeal the Black Papers had routed the liberal consensus in the 1970s (Jones, 1983). Conservative curriculum policies remain potent if often unpublicized. They are likely to have the support not only of parents in Tory areas, but of the poor as well, for mainstream schooling may be competitive, but seems to offer some hope for children to compete for jobs in the shrinking market for labour.

There is, however, another reason why it is misleading to concentrate on the innovatory and radical and to ignore the strength of conservative curriculum policies. There is no straight line from formulating policies to implementing them (Shipman, 1984). Elected members have to work through their officers. CEOs can advise on the basis not only of the legal, financial and administrative position, but on their knowledge of the way teachers and lecturers feel about policies. Even when the Education Committee has adopted the policy it has to be implemented. The path is tortuous. At every stage, administrators, clerks, advisers, inspectors, governors and headteachers adapt and adjust to make the policy fit the reality as seen by those in the very different contexts of county and town hall, local office, school and college. When the door closes on classroom or lecture hall, the half a million teachers and lecturers complete the adaptation. That is why so many policies have had so little impact. It is the history of curriculum innovation. The weakness was not in design, but in the failure to implement in a form recognizable to the designers.

Throughout this account the emphasis has been on the political nature of LEA curriculum policies. Resources are always scarce and their allocation is the subject of pressures for very different curricula. But the political context has changed. The consensus of the 1950s and early 1960s broke with the Labour Party's decision to force the end of selective secondary schooling. With local government increasingly reflecting national party alignments, consensus also disappeared from county and town hall (Jennings, 1977). In the election following local government reorganization in 1974, Independents were decimated. This increased party political influence over curricular issues. The majority party group often meets in advance of the Education Committee to decide policies and tactics. But these groups also tend to be radical left, or Thatcherite right wing. They are now pressing their own policies, as in the case of the ILEA initiatives described earlier. These party groups are often determined to cut through what is seen as a cosy partnership of CEO and teachers, and to force changes that may be uncomfortable for the professionals involved. This, with the influence of corporate management in many LEAs, is very likely to mark the end of the 'great' CEOs such as Clegg in the West Riding who could press for curriculum developments within a relaxed relationship with elected members (Hogan, 1970).

The political dimension within LEAs suggests that the resolution of contrary interests is the key to understanding curricular policy-making. This is rarely dramatic, always involves incremental changes and can be conceptualized along three dimensions. First, there is a continuous interaction between professional and legal factors. Second, there are top-down, bottom-up and lateral, community pressures on LEAs. Third, policies may be radical or conservative. LEAs are organized to accommodate these differing influences. Political members, administrators and advisers bring different views to bear. The administration is often bound into corporate management within the local authority. LEAs are always constrained by financial stringency. They always face the temptation of making policies that will not be implemented. Yet LEAs are proactive as well as reactive. They are politically untidy, yet this allows diverse interests, including teachers, a say in the determination of curriculum policy. Political members have the ultimate say in policy-making, but the diversity in action reflects the many partners able to influence events in classroom, school and LEA.

REFERENCES

Auld Report (1976) *The William Tyndale Junior and Infant Schools*, Inner London Education Authority, London.
Bell, L. and Highman, D. (1984) Curriculum review and curriculum balance, *School Organisation*, **4**, 2.
Birley, D. (1970) *The Education Officer and his World*, Routledge & Kegan Paul, London.
Bullock Report (1975) *A Language for Life*, HMSO, London.
Coe, J. (1974) Signs of the future, *Froebel Journal*, Autumn.
Coventry Education Committee (1976) *Report of a Working Party for the Review of Educational Needs of 14–19 year olds*, Education Department, Coventry.
Coventry Education Committee (1977) *Preventive Social Work in Primary Schools*, Education Department, Coventry.
Coventry Education Committee (1981) *The Education of 11 to 19 year olds*, Education Department, Coventry.
Coventry Education Committee (1983) *Comprehensive Education for Life*, Education Department, Coventry.

DES (1979) *Local Authority Arrangements for the School Curriculum—Report on the Circular 14/77 Review*, HMSO, London.
DES (1980) *A Framework for the School Curriculum*, HMSO, London.
DES (1981) *The School Curriculum*, HMSO, London.
Doe, R. (1981) Framework for a common curriculum, *Times Educational Supplement*, 17 July.
Durham, M. (1984) News, *Times Educational Supplement*, 12 October.
Fowler, G. (1979) The politics of education, in Bernbaum, G., *Schooling in Decline*, Macmillan, Basingstoke.
Giles, R. (1977) *The West Indian Experience in British Schools*, Heinemann, London.
Gipps, C. and Goldstein, H. (1983) *Monitoring Children: an evaluation of the Assessment of Performance Unit*, Heinemann, London.
Gipps, C., Steadman, S., Blackstone, T. and Stierer, B. (1983) *Testing Children: standardised testing in local education authorities and schools*, Heinemann, London.
Hogan, J. M. (1970) *Beyond the Classroom*, Education Explorers, London.
Hough, J. R. (ed.) (1984) *Educational Policy*, Croom Helm, London.
Howell, D. A. and Brown, R. (1983) *Educational Policy Making*, Heinemann, London.
Inner London Education Authority (1969, 1972, 1975, 1977) *Literacy Survey*, Reports to the Schools Sub-Committee, ILEA, London.
Inner London Education Authority (1975) *Literacy Survey: 1973–4 follow-up—preliminary report*, ILEA, Schools Sub-Committee, London.
Inner London Education Authority (1977) *Keeping the School under Review*, ILEA, London.
Inner London Education Authority (1982) *Equal Opportunities for Girls and Boys*, ILEA, London.
Inner London Education Authority (1983) *Anti-Sexist Initiatives in ILEA Schools*, ILEA, London.
Inner London Education Authority (1983) *Race, Sex and Class*, Nos. 1–5, ILEA, London.
Inner London Education Authority (1984) *Is Your School Changing?* ILEA, London.
Jennings, R. E. (1977) *Education and Politics: policy-making in local education authorities*, Batsford, London.
Jones, K. (1983) *Beyond Progressive Education*, Macmillan, London.
Kogan, M. and Packwood, T. (1974) *Advisory Committees and Councils in Education*, Routledge & Kegan Paul, London.
Mann, J. F. (1979) *Education*, Pitman, London.
Passmore, B. (1983) ILEA guidelines on racism anger teachers' unions, *Times Educational Supplement*, 4 November.
Ranson, S. (1980) Changing relations between centre and locality in education, *Local Government Studies*, **6**, 6.
Salter, B. and Tapper, T. (1981) *Education, Politics and the State*, Grant McIntyre, London.
Shipman, M. D. (1982) Commentary on Block 2, E364, *Curriculum Evaluation and Assessment in Educational Institutions*, Open University, Milton Keynes.
Shipman, M. D. (1984) *Education as a Public Service*, Harper & Row, London.
Shipman, M. D., Bolam, D. and Jenkins, D. (1974) *Inside a Curriculum Project*, Methuen, London.
Simon, B. (1981) The primary school revolution: myth or reality, in Simon, B. and Wilcocks, J., *Research and Practice in the Primary School Classroom*, Routledge & Kegan Paul, London.
Venning, P. (1983) Narrow and proud of it, *Times Educational Supplement*, 4 November.
Wood, N. (1983) Head quits because of ILEA "zealots", *Times Educational Supplement*, 30 December.

5

Improving Secondary Schools

INNER LONDON EDUCATION AUTHORITY

[In 1983 the elected members of the Education Committee of the ILEA set up an independent committee of inquiry to consider the curriculum and organization of LEA secondary schools as they affect pupils mainly in the age range of 11-16, with special reference to pupils who are underachieving. The Committee was later asked to pay particular attention to working class children. The Committee, which was chaired by Dr David Hargreaves, reported in February 1984.]

3.11 THE FOURTH AND FIFTH YEARS: ORGANIZING AND ASSESSING THE CURRICULUM

3.11.1 It is in the fourth year that pupils begin serious work on the public examinations syllabuses, which are designed to last for two years. Teachers and other adults can easily forget that two years seems an exceptionally long time to a 14-year-old. As they enter the fourth year pupils are told about the examinations which lie ahead, and that they must begin and maintain hard work. But for many pupils of this age the target is too distant to have reality. Furthermore, sociological studies show that middle-class pupils tend to adapt more easily to long-term goals than some working-class pupils, whose social circumstances so often demand attention to more immediate goals. To this extent, the very structure of the two-year courses disadvantages many working-class pupils. We therefore need to find ways of motivating pupils which do not rely on appeals to goals two years ahead. Additionally, numerous pupils have told us that the examination pressure tends to occur 'in a rush' towards the end of the fifth year, and have criticized the leisurely pace at which their courses began. In our view this is not entirely the fault of teachers. It is simply that, halfway through the fifth year, pupils begin to perceive the goals as real and teachers, recognizing this change in pupil motivation, start to exert more pressure.

3.11.2 At present, pupils following two-year examination courses are forced into excessively passive roles, and not solely as a consequence of didactic

Source: From *Improving Secondary Schools* (Hargreaves Report) (1984), ILEA, London.

teaching methods, for following a public examination syllabus constrains both teacher and pupils to adapt to that syllabus—which seems to allow little choice or control to either party. The principle of 'the negotiated curriculum' may be appropriate to courses of further education, but how far is it realistic in relation to CSE or O Level courses? Indeed, we have recommended a reduction in the present number of options pupils are expected to take, and that in itself will reduce the number of choices available to pupils.

3.11.3 Teachers also face the problem of pupil allocation to courses. Some schools require pupils to choose between CSE and O Level courses at the end of the third year. They recognize that this selection is not always well-founded and may be premature. Moreover, with the apparent devaluation of CSE qualifications in the light of growing youth unemployment, the effect of advising a pupil to take a CSE rather than an O Level course can be demotivating. Other schools, rightly in our view, seek to postpone differentiation into CSE or O Level courses until later, sometimes very much later. But we appreciate that this is never easy and the problems raised by pupils wishing to transfer between CSE and O Level courses are familiar to most schools.

3.11.4 There is also the problem of those pupils who are entered for few or no public examinations at all. One pupil in every five leaves school without any public examination passes, and more than one in three with only one or more 'low grades'. In some cases, pupils have not embarked upon any examination courses at the beginning of the fourth year. The greater number have withdrawn from examination courses at some point during the two years. Inevitably they tend to feel failures and their motivation drops dramatically—especially as they have nothing to show for their efforts or achievements up to this point. Lack of motivation leads to underachievement; lack of achievement further depresses motivation; and a cycle of failure and frustration is established. Such pupils often start to truant or to behave disruptively, exacerbating their underachievement.

3.11.5 Both the O Level and the CSE examination systems continue to be heavily biased towards the assessment of written performance and the reproduction of information with little and, on the whole, only token recognition of the needs of the learner and the processes and skills by which knowledge has been acquired. Whilst the emphasis on coursework evident in many CSE Mode 3 courses is a worthy attempt to redress the balance, and offers scope for more appropriate course content and pedagogy, our impression is that this is not an entirely satisfactory solution: the examination grades are related to CSE Mode 1 and O Level grades and continue to exclude the bottom 40 per cent of pupils from achieving results which are perceived as worthwhile.

3.11.6 Additionally, we believe that too little account is taken of the demands upon pupils made by syllabuses which require coursework folders, field trip reports, special projects, and examinations requiring multiple choice and oral assessments. The production and preservation of course and project work folders requires a degree of self-organization for which many pupils have been unprepared by their earlier years of schooling. Where pupils are following a large number of CSE examination courses, it is understandable that a sizeable proportion of them soon feel overwhelmed by the sheer bulk of paperwork involved, anticipate that their chances of success are small, and consequently abandon their efforts.

3.11.7 It is these problems, amongst others, which have led so many to be critical of the 16 plus examinations. There is a growing recognition that reform is needed. However, the current public examination system will continue for the immediate future and we must make our proposals for development and change on that assumption. We must also take account of another factor. The ILEA in 1982 (ILEA 3524) made its own proposals for change. It is proposed that all pupils should be provided at the age of 16, with a portfolio (The London Record of Achievement) which would contain three elements: results of public examinations (where appropriate); results of graded tests/assessments and a profile or record of achievement. It suggested a programme of work on criterion-referenced graded tests to complement the norm-referenced public examinations. Criterion-referenced graded tests are already well developed in certain areas, such as modern languages, music and typing, and it is held that they have a powerful motivating effect on pupils. One of the advantages of graded tests or, as we would prefer to call them, *graded assessments,* is that they can be adapted to meet the short-term perspectives of many pupils: a series of several levels of graded tests/assessments can complement or replace the two-year course assessment comprising a single examination at the end. Graded tests/assessments are thus easily adapted to the needs of pupils with different abilities and skills and changing levels of motivation, for the tests/assessments can be taken at different rates. The Authority's programme on graded tests/assessments focuses initially on four areas: mathematics; language (English and modern languages); science; and craft, design and technology. We are firmly in favour of these developments.

Leaving certificates and profiles

3.11.8 Account must also be taken of the Authority's innovative work on leaving certificates and profiles. On our visits to schools we have seen for ourselves some of this work and have been greatly impressed by it. The impulse for this innovation has been the teachers' concern to offer to older pupils, especially those who achieve little or nothing in public examinations, a proper record of their achievements in secondary education. These school leaving certificates or profiles escape one of the most unhappy features of most public examination awards, namely the reduction of several years' work to a numerical grade based on a single examination taken at the age of 16. Instead they offer a more detailed and more comprehensive account of achievements, and often include extra-curricular and out-of-school achievements as well as personal qualities. These records of achievement are usually seen to be more fair by pupils, parents and teachers as well as potentially more useful and relevant to employers. The production of these certificates and profiles is costly to the teachers: considerable time and effort is needed if the final outcome is to meet the needs of pupils, and at the same time, to promote a more effective system of record-keeping within the school.

3.11.9 In November 1983 the Secretary of State, Sir Keith Joseph, issued a draft policy statement which aims to develop portfolios on a national level. In January 1984, in his speech at Sheffield, the Secretary of State enlarged on this statement in a way which is highly supportive of the Authority's 1982 proposals and also consonant with the proposals of this Committee. Over the following five years 10 million pounds is to be spent on pilot schemes in six local authorities to provide a foundation for the national introduction of pupils' records. It is clear that these developments, both local and national, will have a profound influence on the curriculum, teaching, record-keeping and organization of secondary schools, especially (but not exclusively) in the fourth and fifth years. In our view the development of portfolios, with graded tests, profiles and other records of achievements, cannot simply be *added onto* the existing practice of schools. The change will need to be more fundamental than this and, if an undue burden is not to be placed on teachers, a careful reappraisal of years three to five of secondary education is required. The efforts and energies of teachers must be carefully channelled and co-ordinated to create a speedy outcome in which changes in curriculum, organization, teaching methods and assessment are welded into a coherent whole. In current educational developments there is a tendency to separate these four dimensions, and we believe this should be resisted.

A proposal for change

3.11.10 The task is this. How are we to resolve the problems raised elsewhere and also design courses and methods of recording which permit a combination of public examination courses, graded tests and profiles/records of achievement, and do so *in a manner which is economical in terms of teachers' time and efforts*? We believe that a critical change is the restructuring of the two-year courses in the fourth and fifth years into *half-term units*. Instead of setting out on a vague two-year educational journey towards nebulous and distant goals, pupils should, from the beginning of the fourth year embark on a series of six to eight week learning units, each of which has a more readily defined and perceived purpose, content, and method of recording. The two-year course would thus be subdivided into 11 or 12 interconnected units, each of which is meaningful in itself and adapted to the time perspective of 14-year-olds, and especially many of those with a working class background. Indeed, there are precedents in university, polytechnic and adult education which suggest that a curriculum organized around shorter-term objectives appeals to *all* learners, regardless of age, sex, class and ethnicity.

3.11.11 A half-term unit permits a form of pupil involvement which is very difficult to achieve in a two-year course. The syllabus content is relatively small, so the pupils can see clearly the knowledge and skills they need to acquire over the next few weeks. Course objectives, instead of existing only in the teacher's mind or the course design, can now be shared with the pupils. If pupils see clearly where they are going, they are more likely to be motivated to make the journey. Once unit objectives have been shared between teacher and pupil, it is easier for teacher and pupil to negotiate the *means* by which unit goals can be reached. In other words, there can be joint planning of methods and procedures of work. This takes pupils out of passive roles into active and collaborative roles with the teacher. At the end of the unit, teachers and pupils can overtly and jointly evaluate the extent to which unit objectives have been achieved. This helps to motivate pupils for the beginning of the next unit. It also makes it genuinely possible for the pupils to play an active role in curriculum development and evaluation.

3.11.12 At the end of each unit, all pupils can be offered a clear and tangible assessment: each unit must give the pupil 'something to show' for the six to eight weeks work. In other words, we believe that some form of assessment should be devised for *every* area of the curriculum in the immediate future. The unit *credit* may take a variety of forms. It might be a certificate which specifies the ground covered and what has been achieved. The advantage here is that pupils can be shown the certificate at the beginning of the unit and thus be made aware of the unit content and have a clear target to aim for. Alternatively the unit credit might be a graded test/assessment or profile. In developing unit credits, each school can draw upon its own experience and preferences and also the distinctive needs of different subjects, whilst also taking account of developments relating to the London Record of Achievement (which we see as complementary to our proposals) as well as innovations arising from DES initiatives. Whatever the format of the unit credit, its existence will, we believe, enhance pupil motivation for the unit as well as for the succeeding units, since the units are cumulative. Moreover, the unit credit is a permanent record of achievement (and the quality of the credit format should reflect this) so that even if a pupil does not ultimately enter for a public examination, the credit remains. It is essential that pupils see the potential value of the credit for use in seeking employment and/or for entry into further education. The credit also serves as a form of school record, which can be the basis for reports to parents. Thus the unit credit can serve several purposes.

3.11.13 The concept of the unit credit allows teachers to capitalize on one of the most important developments within schools in recent years, namely a much more sophisticated approach to the assessment of pupils. One of the most important aspects in the emergence of profiles is the new role that is allocated to the pupil in assessment. The best work has shown that assessment is not merely something which flows unidirectionally from teacher to pupil, but a joint enterprise in which pupil self-assessment plays a vital part. We strongly commend this approach. Pupils' commitment is likely to be strengthened when they take some real responsibility, in discussion with the teachers, for monitoring their own progress, recognizing strengths, detecting weaknesses, and devising strategies for improvement. The unit credit should in our view contain, or be accompanied by, such diagnostic and self-assessment materials, which can be made known to parents so that they can play a more informed and supportive part in promoting the education of their children. Units and credits should be an important topic for discussion on parents' evenings and at meetings of our proposed tutor group parents' associations. The more parents understand the details of curriculum content and methods of assessment, the more likely they are to act in partnership with teachers to foster pupil motivation and hard work. The unit credit also allows more attention to the practical or applied aspects of a course of study. In our view all unit credits should make explicit reference to the assessment of relevant practical or applied knowledge and skills.

3.11.14 The problem of allocation of pupils to O Level and CSE courses may be eased by the unit scheme. Some of the units, especially those in the early part of the fourth year, may be common to both public examinations, especially when the syllabuses overlap. Some units, especially those in later terms, may be more specific to a particular examination. If the units are carefully designed, the decision about examination entry may be postponed until a later date than is the current practice of some ILEA schools. Some pupils will not ultimately be entered for a public examination in a subject. Whilst units will need to be specially designed for such pupils, these can be readily added on to the previous units. As a result, there will be a less obvious segregation of some pupils as 'non-examination' pupils and it should prove easier to maintain their motivation. And those pupils who perform badly in the public examination will have their file of unit credits which will give a fairer and fuller picture of past achievements than a low grade CSE. These credits should prove very useful for pupils when they enter further education. By the fifth year it will be apparent that some pupils are covering too wide a range of studies. It is possible for these pupils to abandon some of the subjects within our suggested 'free options' and instead take additional units in the compulsory subjects so that their achievements can be enhanced within a somewhat narrower range. Some pupils need more time than others on certain subjects and the unit scheme has the flexibility to accommodate the needs of such pupils.

3.11.15 In some subject areas a considerable amount of work has recently taken place on restructuring examination syllabuses in ways that are consonant with our proposals for a system of units and credits. One example is the South London Consortium's CSE Mode 3 English syllabus. The syllabus comprises 10 course modules together with suggestions for written assignments and detailed advice relating to assessment. Assessment of oral skills counts for 25 per cent of the final mark and has two components, an oral test, and continuous oral assessment so that credit can be given for those oral abilities difficult to assess effectively in the test. We commend this syllabus as an illustration of the approach to fourth and fifth year work we would like to see adopted in other curriculum subjects, although we would add a caution that in any reorganization of a syllabus into a modular or unit system, care should be taken to include attention to all communication skills *within* each module or unit.

3.11.16 We believe it is within the power of all ILEA secondary schools to restructure the fourth and fifth years along the lines we have proposed. It would, of course, require much time and effort from the teachers. Whilst some schools might wish to go no further than this, others could use the unit scheme as a step towards a larger reform of the fourth and fifth years. The division of courses into units permits a degree of pupil choice between units. Most courses are not neatly 'linear', requiring each unit to be taken in a predetermined sequence. In a medium sized or large school it should be possible to allow pupils some choice over the sequence in which units are taken. This possibility for granting greater choice to pupils is increased if the school is willing to mix fourth and fifth year pupils for some of the time, so that some units are open to *both* fourth and fifth year pupils. Many examination syllabuses now permit a degree of choice. If the fourth and fifth years are mixed, it might be possible for teachers to offer a wider curriculum content than at present and so allow pupils to exercise choice according to their own interests, needs and aspirations. There are other advantages to mixing the fourth and fifth years. By selecting an appropriate combination of units, the most able pupils can follow an accelerated course and be entered for a public examination at the end of the fourth year, which can serve to encourage these pupils as well as reducing the pressure on them when most subjects are taken at the end of the fifth year. Mixing the fourth and fifth years can also give much greater flexibility to small schools, or schools that have been badly affected by rapidly falling rolls. Intead of having to provide a separate curriculum for each year group of say, 90 pupils, combining the fourth and fifth years permits the development of a unified curriculum for 180 pupils.

3.11.17 Whether or not the fourth and fifth years are mixed, block timetabling by subject can be used to give pupils some choice between different units or the sequence of units. Whilst there is always a danger of presenting young people with too many choices, we believe that in most schools pupils need more, not fewer, opportunities for making choices. We recognize that our proposals for the fourth and fifth year curriculum as a whole involve a reduction in pupil choice *between* subjects, since we advocate an increase in the common curriculum with a consequent reduction in the number of options. Block timetabling and/or mixing of the fourth and fifth years, when combined with our unit scheme, permits pupil choice *within* a subject area and we believe a degree of choice here is essential if pupil motivation and responsibility is to be maximized.

3.11.18 The scheme we have outlined has implications for the curriculum and organization of third year teaching. We believe some schools might wish to reconsider the third year in order to make it a better preparation for the fourth and fifth year curriculum and organization we have proposed.

We recommend that:

● *headteachers,* in consultation with teachers, review the curriculum and timetable for fourth and fifth years and develop a system of units and unit credits.

6

The Content and Context of Educational Reform

DAVID RAFFE

CONTENT AND CONTEXT

There is a tendency among some commentators to dismiss the concept of individual choice within the education system and to present all behaviour as subject to external control, whether this is achieved through internalized norms or through more overt forms of coercion. This view, we believe, is mistaken and misleading. By ignoring the scope for individual choice within education systems, and the extent to which individuals make decisions which are reasonable for them, this view neglects a principal source of structural constraint on change.

The school system offers opportunities for choice at several stages of the school career. During compulsory secondary schooling the main choices formally offered to pupils are through the subject-options system at the beginning of third year. The scope for pupil choice is restricted here, especially with respect to the level at which courses are taken. However, there is a second and possibly more important area of choice available to pupils during compulsory schooling, although it is not formally recognized as such by the school system. This is the choice of whether or not to take courses seriously, to attend regularly, and to comply whole-heartedly with the academic and behavioural demands of the school. Further choices open up at 16, when pupils may enter the labour market or the Youth Training Scheme,

Source: From Raffe, D. (1984) *Fourteen to Eighteen*, Aberdeen University Press, Aberdeen.

go on to further education, or stay on at school: and if they stay on they are likely to face a widening range of choices especially between academic and vocational courses. Those who complete fifth year must choose whether or not to start a sixth; and the best qualified leavers can choose whether or not to apply to higher education. Young people, therefore, face several types of choices as they progress through the school system. What is important for our present argument is that all the policy initiatives we have discussed aim to influence young people's decisions with respect to one or more of these types of choices.

In our analyses we have seen that young people, when faced with these choices, often make decisions that are highly predictable, given knowledge of such circumstances as their attainment, social background and local conditions. However, this does not mean that they have no real choice: the minority who go against the general pattern are proof that the scope for choice exists. Nor is the predictability of most decisions necessarily evidence of a lack of deliberation or rationality or free will. Rather we would argue that this predictability reflects the tendency for most young people to make decisions that respect and follow the (predictable) logic of the situations in which they find themselves.

Young people may share norms and perceptions which help to define these situations and suggest appropriate courses of action; they may be influenced by advice, shared values and assumptions, and other pressures from family, peer group and school; their decision-making may sometimes be confused, and at other times their behaviour may be the result of non-decisions, taken by default. It is also true that some young people make decisions which they (or others) later judge to be 'wrong'. Nevertheless, the conclusion that flows, overwhelmingly, from our discussion is that young people are not passive and unreasoning puppets, manipulated by convention or coercion. However muddled the processes which lead to their decisions may sometimes appear to be, the resulting behaviours do tend to observe and to follow the logic of their situation; and we must understand this situation if we are to understand the present or future behaviour of young people in an education system.

It is this situation and this logic that we refer to as 'context'. To a large extent it is constituted by the structure of selection and differentiation within the education system and by its relation to differentiation within the labour market and within society as a whole. Young people's educational decisions tend to be forward-looking; they are influenced not only by the more immediate, intrinsic considerations (such as liking the subject or the teacher), but also by considerations of longer-term advantage. Their decisions therefore reflect judgements about the routes through the maze of educational and occupational selection which are most likely to lead young people to their eventual goals. These goals are often directly or indirectly vocational. Frequently [in this study] we have seen how at successive decision points young people are influenced by considerations to do with jobs and employment. Even when they choose between alternatives within education, such as third-year options or different kinds of post-compulsory education, they often choose on the basis of occupational criteria. These criteria may be specific, relating to particular occupational aspirations, or general, relating to the desire for a 'good' or well paid (or sometimes for any) job. This is not to deny that young people are also influenced by those hierarchies of esteem that are largely internal to the education system; but the disinterested scholar, motivated solely by a love of learning, is a rare figure in Scottish education.

We would argue that young people's decisions are influenced less by the *content* of the available educational provision—its intrinsic educational quality or relevance—than by its *context* and in particular by the relation of provision to the structure of educational and occupational selection. However, as we have observed, current policy initiatives depend for their success upon their power to influence young people's decisions. These initiatives variously aim to improve motivation and behaviour during compulsory schooling, to increase overall participation within post-compulsory education, or to induce students—the 'right' students—to enter particular types of courses. Their success depends upon the decisions of young people, which in turn are influenced by context. It follows that educational policies, even if they are primarily concerned with changing the content of education, must also take account of its context.

A recurring theme of this study is that many educational policies fail to achieve their objectives because, although they pay considerable attention to the content of educational provision, they take insufficient account of its context. This is not to say that problems arising from the context of educational provision are easily solved. Indeed the nature of these problems is such that a balance must always be struck between competing objectives; elsewhere these conflicts have been described in terms of the related problems of difficulty, selection and motivation (Gray *et al.*, 1983, pp. 7–14). Nor do we argue that policy-makers wholly ignore context; both the Munn/Dunning reforms and the Action Plan can be thought of as attempts to influence young people's decisions by reshaping the context of their choices. However, as we suggest below, the view of context underlying these initiatives tends to be narrow in scope and inadequate for reconciling the conflicting purposes of policy and for overcoming powerful structural obstacles to change. Moreover, the process of development and the testing of initiatives encourages this bias towards content: it is standard practice to pilot the content of new courses, but it is almost impossible to pilot their context. The backgrounds and interests of educational innovators also predispose them to think in terms of content. The focus of teacher education is on the purpose and content of education, not on the ways in which existing school systems provide differentiated pathways through the educational structure and into the labour market. Unlike pupils and parents, educationists have mistrusted instrumental views of education (Morton-Williams and Finch, 1968); they have particularly mistrusted vocational instrumentalism as this is seen to threaten their largely child-centred view of education. Unfortunately, the tenable opinion that context *should* not be important often leads to a false judgement that context *is* not important and that it can be ignored.

The tendency of policy-makers to think in terms of 'modal groups' illustrates a narrow view of context and neglects the extent to which pupils and students, sometimes guided by their teachers, act in the light of wider considerations of context. The O-grade was designed for 30 per cent of pupils; but more than twice as many eventually took it. The CSYS was expected to attract intending university entrants and others who had acquired the qualifications necessary to their plans by the end of fifth year; but large numbers of them either left school after fifth year or devoted their sixth year to improving their Highers record. Throughout our study—in the Munn and Dunning reforms, in the official interpretation of staying-on rates, and above all in the bewildering tangle of opportunities at 16-plus—we have seen examples of a close and often admirable attention to the details of content thwarted by inadequate or inappropriate attention to the context.

FOURTEEN TO SIXTEEN

Several factors determine the context of educational choices made before the age of 16. Schooling is compulsory; the range of options is therefore restricted, and no option offers any immediate pecuniary advantage to the student. Decision points are related almost entirely to stage, rather than age. Although stage and age may be out of step for many pupils, this has little bearing on the nature or the outcomes of the choices at 14. Decisions made at 14, however, are influenced by their anticipated consequences for selection at 16 or later; the earlier decisions are therefore influenced by the logic of anticipated future ones. When selectors (especially employers) choose among students who have taken different options within a hierarchically differentiated curriculum, they tend to select those who have taken the options with the highest status in the hierarchy, rather than those who have taken the options whose content they judge most suitable. Employers tend to ask not 'how relevant is the curriculum that this student has just mastered?' but 'how good was this student in order to enter this course?' (For evidence of this see CPRS, 1980, pp. 4–5, and Gray *et al.*, 1983, chapter 7.) This means that selection decisions at one stage in a young person's career (e.g. at 16) may be based directly or indirectly on selection decisions at an earlier stage (at 14); the earlier decisions must anticipate this effect. We call this anticipatory self-selection.

In the last two years of compulsory schooling a number of pupils plan their courses on the assumption that they will stay on for a fifth year; others assume they will leave at 16 and may therefore view choices in a shorter-term vocational perspective. Despite this, up to the age of 16 the hierarchy of educational differentiation tends to be unambiguous and unique. By and large the kinds of choices and attainments which are optimal do not depend on the ambitions of the pupil. In concrete terms this means that good attainment in public examinations at 16, and a diet of the more academic subjects, is of probable future benefit whether a pupil wishes to continue with full-time education after 16 or whether he or she wishes to leave at 16 and look for a job. This means, for example, that there is little in the context of education as it is presently organized to force a choice between academic and vocational streams at 14; on extrinsic grounds, most pupils would be advised to remain in the academic one if they can.

The fact that education up to the age of 16 is characterized by a unique hierarchy of attainment and advantage is critical for the future of the Munn and Dunning reforms. The strategy is based upon the promise of 'prizes for everyone'. The logic of this strategy is only viable if there are many different competitions and if each pupil is capable of success in at least one of them. Such an approach is consistent with the notion advanced by a number of commentators that comprehensive education should attempt to develop, and reward, competence in a much wider range of fields than the cognitive or academic skills that it currently esteems (Gatherer, 1980; Ryrie, 1981; Hargreaves, 1982). However, for this approach to work, each area of competition must be perceived as both valid and worthwhile; but this is unlikely. For the present context of 14–16 education indicates that one type of competition, one dimension of attainment, is of overwhelming importance on the criteria that count with most pupils; and the Munn and Dunning plans do not attempt to eliminate this aspect of context. They seek, instead, to extend it and systematize it by relating the difficulty of courses more closely to ability. Two considerations help to explain the limitations of the Munn and Dunning proposals. First, as we have noted above, the structural logic of educational context means that policy-makers cannot fully realize all policy objectives simultaneously, but must find a compromise among them. Second, the terms of reference of the two reports restricted them to reforming only those aspects of context that were internal to the third and fourth years of secondary schooling. Patterns of subsequent selection, in post-compulsory education and in the labour market, were outside this remit.

To the extent that the problems which Munn and Dunning sought to redress were created by the context of education rather than by its content we therefore see little reason to expect the new reforms to solve them. For example, we anticipate strong pressures from pupils and parents for over-presentation at Credit level, just as there were strong pressures for over-presentation at O-grade. We anticipate similar pressures at the borderline between Foundation and General. This trend is likely to be accentuated by the evidence that D or E awards at O-grade, though widely regarded as 'fail' grades, nevertheless significantly influence employment chances: a finding which almost certainly means that O-grade presentations and not only results can be important. In the post-Dunning situation this suggests that merely attempting a Credit (rather than a General) or a General (rather than a Foundation) will have occupational value: more encouragement to over-presentation. Further encouragement will be provided by the knowledge that after starting courses in many subjects it may be possible to transfer downwards but only exceptionally to move up to a higher level of course.

In similar vein we doubt if the mere extension of certification to include pupils on the new Foundation courses can totally remove their low motivation and feelings of exclusion from the moral community of the school. Such pupils will be well aware that their prizes are of little more than nominal value, the wooden spoons of the Scottish educational race. Yet our scepticism is itself qualified. The introduction of Foundation awards will at least give pupils something to work for; a Foundation certificate will presumably be better than no certificate. Equally important, the performance of schools will now be publicly certifiable at all ability levels; the extension of certification might reduce the pressure on schools to concentrate limited resources on the abler (and formerly certificate) pupils at the expense of the others. This of course depends on whether the three Dunning levels are perceived as of equal importance within the educational community and among pupils and parents.

We also doubt whether the Munn and Dunning reforms can abolish the status hierarchy of subjects, not least because this hierarchy is deeply embedded in the context of 14–16 education as a result both of subsequent occupational and educational selection and of the values and organization of the secondary schools themselves. Indeed the persistence of this hierarchy is evident in the more recent Munn and Dunning proposals. Some critics have alleged that 'the proposed curriculum is no more than a crude device for differentiating pupils on the single dimension of ability in the "cognitive intellectual" subjects' (Drever et al., 1983, p. 4). This drift in the policy process—the subversion of Munn by Dunning—is evidence less of an ideologically based conspiracy than of coming to terms with a context of selection based on such a hierarchy.

More generally, throughout the Munn and Dunning debate one can detect a conflict between the anti-hierarchical tradition which seeks to develop the 'whole child', and the more practically oriented approach which tends to accept the hierarchical assumptions that it finds embedded in present practice but seeks to make their application more efficient and fair. Every major change in the organisation of secondary schooling could be related to these two perspectives. Thus, on the one hand, moves to lengthen the period of compulsory schooling, a campaign which has had a wide consensus of support throughout this century, could be seen as an attempt to extend the time spent in the protected environment of the school in which children could be free to develop their general education unfettered by the demands of the labour market. From the more pragmatic and achievement-oriented perspective, on the other hand, it could be said that one of the most important features of the latest stage of that long campaign, the RSLA decision of 1972, was that it guaranteed for (almost) all pupils the opportunity to compete for public accreditation within the period of compulsory schooling. Aspects of the Munn/Dunning programme which most clearly reflect the anti-hierarchical tradition—for example the attempt to broaden the curriculum of all pupils and to introduce more flexible school-based assessment into all examination courses—were under threat from the outset. As the Munn and Dunning proposals have made the transition from general philosophy to specific practical proposals, it is the hierarchical view, reinforced by the context of education, which has gained the upper hand.

REFERENCES

Central Policy Review Staff (1980) *Education, Training and Industrial Performance*, HMSO, London.

Drever, E. *et al.* (1983) A response to 'A Framework for Decision', Department of Education, University of Stirling, Stirling, (mimeo).

Gatherer, W. (1980) Educating the 16s to 19s: choices and costs, in *Choice, Compulsion and Cost*, HMSO, Edinburgh.

Gray, J., McPherson, A. F. and Raffe, D. (1983) *Reconstructions of Secondary Education: theory, myth and practice since the War*, Routledge & Kegan Paul, London.

Hargreaves, D. H. (1982) *The Challenge for the Comprehensive School: culture, curriculum and community*, Routledge & Kegan Paul, London.

Morton-Williams, R. and Finch, S. (1968) *Young School Leavers: Schools Council Enquiry 1*, HMSO, London.

Ryrie, A. C. (1981) *Routes and Results*, Hodder & Stoughton for SCRE, Sevenoaks.

7

Towards a Tertiary Tripartism
new codes of social control and the 17+

STEWART RANSON

Since 1945 there have been two remarkable transformations[1] of education designed, arguably, to produce and reproduce fundamentally different conceptions of society. This paper is an attempt to throw some light upon aspects of the present restructuring which began in the mid-1970s and is still being developed.

EDUCATION FOR EXPANSION

The first transforming of education began in the late 1950s and saw the development of assumptions and institutions which thrived until the early 1970s. The change was designed to facilitate the regeneration of post-industrial Britain in ways which would lead to a more efficient economy as well as a fairer and more open society. Greatly expanded educational chances would, it was hoped, provide the human capital to fuel economic growth, while increased equality of opportunity would support the disadvantaged and undermine the suffocating constraints of class domination. Educational reform would lead Britain into the modern world. To accomplish such a radical extension of opportunities, fundamental changes would be required in institutions and curriculum, in administration and control. The old outmoded tripartite school system which selected and excluded the majority of young people would need to be remodelled in favour of comprehensive schools that would impose no artificial barriers upon the development of pupils. All would then have access to the same forms of knowledge and

Source: From Broadfoot, P. (ed.) (1984) *Selection, Certification and Control*, Falmer Press, Falmer.

experience that would become the foundation of common life chances. The curriculum as idealized in Plowden (1967), was designed progressively to focus upon the needs of each young person and to foster inquiring, creative capacities through individual discovery and experience. The focus was upon personal development rather than preparation for future economic or vocational roles. The structures of administration and control adjusted to such purposes and tasks with considerable influence accorded to the strategic community of professional teachers in schools.

Demographic and economic growth and, most significantly, political will coalesced in the expansion and transforming of education during this (1955–1975) period. But the forces began to alter fundamentally in the mid-1970s. Education occupied a changed world. School rolls were on the threshold of decline, the economy was entering recession and unemployment, especially amongst the young, was beginning to accelerate. The contraction of resources and the rationalization of institutional provision would become necessary but, most importantly, political conceptions of the purposes and value of education had begun to alter. Beliefs about the contributions which the service might make to economy and society seemed to have been eroded while parents and industrialists questioned the nature and quality of the educational offering. A second restructuring was beginning to take shape.

EDUCATION FOR INDUSTRIAL REGENERATION

The challenge of unemployment and the changing political context brought into focus the relationship of education to the world of work and, in particular, the adequacy of the preparations made by school for the 16–19 age group. Many industrialists argued that schools were too self-absorbed and preoccupied with the social development of young people rather than with preparing them for their economic roles in industry and commerce. The challenges coincided with internal analyses by officials and Her Majesty's Inspectorate at the Department of Education and Science (DES). This work had its (leaked) public expression in 1976 in a memorandum known as the 'Yellow Book' (the work for which had begun as early as 1974). The memorandum argued that the weakness of secondary education was that it underprepared young people for employment: 'the time may now be ripe for change as the national mood and government policies have changed in the face of hard and irreducible facts'.[2] The complaints of employers were noted, that school leavers lacked basic skills in communication and calculation and hence the basic knowledge to benefit from technical training: more practical courses, it was believed, would help to remedy this problem. The needs of the 16–19 age group should be given priority, the Yellow Book argued, especially the less able academically who provide 'a good illustration of the essential principle that education and training must be planned in a unified way if

[they] are to be attracted by courses and to gain practical benefit from them'. The Yellow Book concluded that the vocational relevance of 14–19 provision should be improved by the introduction of more practical courses, by establishing more imaginative links between school and college as well as with the training agencies.

The argument that a fundamental redirection of education was required, and of 14–19 provision in particular, required, possibly, the support and legitimation of ultimate sources of power. Callaghan's premiership initiated and developed this basic review and redirection of the service. His speech at Ruskin College in October 1976 expressed concern that the needs of industry and commerce were not being met by education and called for a national debate on the service. The Green Paper (HMSO, 1977), summarizing the debate, reinforced the themes outlined by the Prime Minister:

> that the school system is geared to promote the importance of academic learning and careers with the result that pupils, especially the more able, are prejudiced against work in productive industry and trade; that teachers lack experience, knowledge and understanding of trade and industry; that curricula are not related to the realities of most pupils' work after leaving school; and that pupils leave school with little or no understanding of the workings, or the importance, of the wealth producing sector of our economy.

The education service was answerable to the society which it served and should therefore be responsive to such criticisms. It was 'vital to Britain's economic recovery and standard of living that the performance of manufacturing industry was improved and that the whole range of government policies, including education, contribute as much as possible to improving industrial performance and thereby increasing national wealth'.

A fundamental redirection of education was given encouragement by senior Whitehall officials as part of their larger review of economic and industrial strategy. The Treasury in particular took the view that education should serve the economic needs of the country: 'we took a strong view that education could play a much better role in improving industrial performance. The service is inefficient, rather unproductive and does not concentrate scarce resources in the areas that matter most. The economic climate and imperatives are clear; the task is to adjust education to them.'[3] The Cabinet Office has been as direct and severe about the service: 'young people should be given a more direct awareness of the probable needs of their future employers. Education has been too isolated and independent of the country's economic needs and in future the output of schools will have to be keyed more tightly into employment needs.'[4]

The driving force for change, however, has not been an external source of influence but the DES itself. The policy of reconstructing the education service has been led by the Department who have championed the initiative of strengthening the ties between school and work, between education and training in order to improve the vocational preparation of the 14–19 age group. Restructuring would require complex changes to key components of the education system: institutions would have to be rationalized, finance

redirected and, critically, the curriculum and examinations would need to be
recast. The DES believed that control of the curriculum was central to its
purpose:

> our focus must be on the strategic questions of the content, shape and purposes of the whole
> educational system and absolutely central to that is the curriculum. We would like
> legislative powers over the curriculum and the powers to control the exam system by ending
> all those independent charters of the exam bodies.[5]

In the absence of such powers, attention focused on the 16–19 sector
because of its strategic location between secondary schooling and the world of
work (or the prospect of unemployment) and, because it was less hedged
around by statutory constraints, it was more amenable to policy initiative and
change. The point was underlined by a senior official:

> the 16–19 area is one of the key means of changing the educational system and of achieving
> the relevance we desire because it sits at the watershed between school and work. If we can
> achieve things with the new 17+ examination that will give us an important lever to
> vocationalise or to re-vocationalise the last years of public schooling. That will be a very
> important, and significant step, indeed.[6]

CURRICULUM DEVELOPMENT FOR THE 17+: CEE, ABC, CPVE

To achieve its objective of introducing a vocational curriculum and
examination at 17, the DES had first to negotiate intricate reforms in both the
schools and the further education sectors. While the problem in schools was
said to be the inappropriateness of the traditional ('academic') offering, the
problem in Further Education (FE) was defined as the need to rationalize a
profusion of courses 'so tangled as to confound the investigator'.[7] Two DES
committees (the Keohane and Mansell committees) would be formed to
clarify the 'client group', define their needs and review courses and modes of
assessment.

In order, however, to understand fully the work of those committees and
the present attempts to develop courses and exams at 17, we need to grasp a
little of the historical context. We need to appreciate that the initiative to
develop the 17+ began, in fact, in the 1960s, that is, during the period of the
first post-war education transformation. An understanding of the earlier
development illuminates the contrast of educational purpose between the two
periods, as well as the longevity of reform in education.

One of the first decisions of the newly created Schools Council in 1964 was
to reappraise the post-16 curriculum in the light of the changing character of
the sixth form and of society in general. The excessive narrowness of
advanced provision and the need to design courses for the 'new sixth former'
were immediate priorities. In 1968 the Council established a working party
led by Dr Briault to examine the curricular needs of young people who
wished to remain at school or college for an extra year of general education.

The working party's reports were published in 1972/73 as Working Papers 45/6.

The Briault committee believed that the 'new sixth' comprised a wide range of abilities and interests and, given the rapidity of social and economic change, the curriculum should be designed to reflect and encourage such diversity: 'schools and colleges will have to plan for diversity, allow for the late developer and the student who changes courses and make sure that no route is a dead end: we attach particular importance to this point—options *must* be kept open wherever possible.'[8] The curriculum, it was proposed, should set a premium upon understanding, encouraging pupils to think and find connections across their studies. The new examinations should foster independence and originality of thought, allowing sufficient scope for the expression of personal qualities such as initiative, imagination and persistence in the carrying out of projects. The curriculum should, nevertheless, be balanced and relevant to the modern world, perhaps considering a vocational 'point of departure', although a common curriculum would be inappropriate to individual choice and need.

Briault proposed a Certificate of Extended Education (CEE) to be developed in a number of pilot schemes in association with the CSE exam boards. In 1976 the Council recommended that the experimental exam become formally recognized by the Secretary of State but neither Mr Mulley nor his successor as Secretary of State for Education, Mrs Williams, was prepared to give consent to CEE before decisions were made about the whole framework of 16–19 examinations and while employers were still expressing doubts about the usefulness of the new exam. In the autumn of 1977 the Secretary of State announced her intention to form the (Keohane) committee to review CEE and its relationship to similar courses provided in FE colleges. The report of the Keohane Committee, *Proposals for a Certificate of Extended Education,* was published in December 1979.[9] Early in 1978 the (Mansell) committee was established by the Further Education Unit (FEU) at the DES to review comparable non-advanced courses in colleges: their report, *A Basis for Choice* (ABC/7), was published in June.[10]

The two committees reviewing courses in the different education sectors came to many similar conclusions which distanced them from the aims and interpretations of the Briault reports. Whereas the earlier review had described diversity of interests and abilities, both the Keohane and Mansell committees believed their 'target groups' to comprise low achieving young people of average ability who need primarily 'to prepare themselves effectively for employment'. Both committees were in agreement about the aims of the curriculum which should develop a vocational orientation that helps 'them understand what employers will expect from them [and] what they should expect from employment': courses should 'encourage the development of a *realistic* vocational focus' (my emphasis). Both committees believed, therefore, that employers needs and demands should acquire

priority in curriculum design. Nevertheless, the Keohane committee conceded that the model for such pre-employment courses lay in the tradition of
Further Education where the distinctive grouped curriculum was designed as
an integration of the elements the providers believed students *should* acquire.
But while Keohane's 'CEE' proposed separate courses leading to exams,
Mansell's 'ABC' proposed one course leading to profile assessment. School
and college would develop vocational preparation courses to suit their own
institutions and traditions.

   While the Secretary of State deliberated upon these two reports, the
disparate interests voiced their competing claims. The Certificate of
Secondary Education (CSE) Exam Boards, the Schools Council and the
teacher unions urged support for the findings of Keohane, while the FE
institutes, the FEU and the National Association of Teachers in Further and
Higher Education (NATFHE) proclaimed the virtues of the Mansell
Report. In October 1980 the Government finally set out its policy in a
consultative paper, 'Examinations 16–18',[11] which recommended in favour of
the FEU report. The Green Paper concluded that 'members of the target
group in both sectors can best be served by provision more akin to traditional
FE developed in the light of *A Basis For Choice*'. Accordingly the
Government proposed that CEE be eliminated expeditiously because it was
insufficiently vocationally oriented and left too much discretion to schools. As
such, the development of the pre-vocational courses would pass to one of the
FE validating bodies (probably the City and Guilds of London Institute
(CGLI)); the General Certificate of Education (GCE) and CSE boards
were to be excluded.

   Such a firm prescriptive decision should, ostensibly, have eliminated
equivocation and established the authority of the Department amidst rival
contending interests. But the schools sector—for example, the CSE boards,
the Schools Council, the National Union of Teachers (NUT) and the
College Principals—led an immediate, vociferous and well orchestrated
challenge against the narrow definition of the student group and its needs,
against what they believed to be manifest steering of young people into
vocational routes without opportunities for educational progression, and
tacitly against arrangements which encroached arbitrarily upon their
financial interests. Effective political support was mobilized for their
demands within the DES which was beginning to fracture according to the
different interests of its internal divisions. Ministers and officials were
beginning to take sides in the confrontation between the education and
training sectors. This organized resistance achieved two important concessions: first, only two months after publication of the Green Paper it was
announced that the CSE boards were to be incorporated in the validation of
the new exam and, second, when the Government finally published the
details of the new 17+ Exam in May 1982[12] the contents had been redrafted
to accommodate schools sector interests. The curriculum would remain

vocationally oriented, retain work experience and continue to prepare young people effectively for employment. But the course was now aimed at students 'with a wide range of interests, expectations and abilities' who need a 'broad programme of general education' that would prepare them for 'adult life' as well as for work. The curriculum would offer a core of basic studies before elective options were chosen in technical, business and general studies: development work in the latter would need to build upon the pioneering work of the CSE and GCE Boards. A Certificate of Pre-Vocational Education (CPVE) would be accorded to all students recording details of performance, although attainment in key aspects—maths, English and science—would have to be externally assessed or moderated.

CONCEPTUALIZING THE CODES OF CURRICULUM CHANGE

The central thrust of the curriculum development inherent in these proposals is to negotiate for schools and colleges a vocational curriculum that will prepare the great majority of so-called 'non-advanced' students for their economic roles in industry and commerce. Priorities and values have shifted: training is preferred to education, practical skills are elevated above understanding, detailed profiles replace impersonal exams, and external control of the curriculum by employers and administrators displaces the influence of the professional community of teachers. How are such changes to the 16–19 curriculum to be understood and what analytical concepts will allow us to interpret their meaning?

In its structuring of selected knowledge and experience the curriculum operates to produce and reproduce a system of values and power in society (Williams, 1961; Bernstein, 1975; Lawton, 1980). This relationship is developed imaginatively in the work of Bernstein and provides an appropriate means of gaining conceptual purchase upon changes to the 17+ curriculum described above. Bernstein proposes that the educational experience of young people is shaped by curricula which define what is to count as valid knowledge and pedagogic processes that determine acceptable forms for the transmission of knowledge. Underlying and unifying the message systems of curriculum and pedagogy are principles or codes which regulate the structure of knowledge ('classification') and the processes of transmission ('framing'). Classification, referring to the extent of differentiation and insulation of curricula contents, seeks to focus attention upon the forms of power which maintain and reproduce the boundaries between categories. Framing, on the other hand, refers to the context in which knowledge is transmitted and by defining the principles which regulate what may be transmitted seeks to conceptualize the underlying principles of control.

Bernstein's typology of educational codes—'collection' and 'integrated' —and the shift he discerns taking place between dominant codes reflects and illuminates the present changes to the 17+ curriculum. Collection codes typify the secondary school curriculum with its purest expression at Advanced Level GCE yet equally reflected in the proposals for a Certificate of Extended Education. The curriculum here reinforced the value of specialized knowledge through compartmentalized subjects. The purity of specialist knowledge is protected not only through the maintenance of subject boundaries but also through the hierarchical ordering of pupils who, streamed and graded, must demonstrate capacity by passing through ritual exams to attain selected membership of more advanced stages. The Keohane allegiance to single examinable subjects sought to reproduce this curricular format in the CEE, and also, therefore, traditional modes of framing. Framing is typically weaker in English education than in many European countries and thus allows a greater variety of teaching styles. Nevertheless, such weak framing grants essential control to teachers who can, didactically, regulate the selection and transmission of educational knowledge.

It is an important characteristic of framing under collection codes that what is being regulated is the pupils' access to realms of knowledge that are detached from the immediacy of everyday life: the universal replaces the particular, the abstract and distant replaces the familiar and common sense. Yet the strength of this framing has often varied with the 'ability' of the pupils, so that the less advanced, slower learning, students are exposed to learning situations much less removed from day-to-day experience. This weak framing, reflected in the construction of the Keohane CEE, is often associated, Bernstein alludes, 'with purposes of social control'.

The dominant modes of control underlying collection codes rest upon principles of academic hierarchy and surveillance, on selective and ritualized socialization and, most significantly, upon the maintenance of strong boundaries which insulate packages of knowledge in ways which render them predictable and controllable. A divided curriculum is a controlled curriculum. Yet differentiated curricula typically create differentiated individuals with varying experiences and specific identities. Because the focus is upon the ordering of knowledge rather than persons (or at least only upon persons indirectly) the spaces within and between boundaries allow individuals privacy, thus reducing 'the penetration of the socialization process, for it is possible to distance oneself from it.'[13]

Yet the invasion of personal privacy is one of the distinctive consequences of a shift in education from collection to integrated codes. Bernstein perceives such a movement taking place in English education, as yet unrealized and incomplete, but exemplified he argues, in the typical 'Plowden-inspired' primary school and in curriculum developments like the Nuffield science project. Bernstein was, therefore, describing and conceptualizing changes which were emerging during the first post-war transformation of education.

Yet the shift to an integrated curriculum is more than ever manifest in the present proposals—during the second phase transformation—for a pre-vocational course and assessment at 17. The paradox of continuity and contrast in coding between the two periods will require analysis below.

An integrated curriculum, as described by Bernstein, is characterized by an openness which 'blurs the boundaries between subjects'.

It is the argument of this paper that the forebodings of Bernstein about the emerging integrated code of the late 1960s are in fact being realized in the developing integrated code of the 1980s, as illustrated in particular in the Keohane or Mansell proposals for a vocational certificate at 17. There are common elements between the codings of the two periods. The overriding theme of vocationalism provides the relational idea which subordinates the distinctiveness of separate subjects and erodes the boundaries which protect their independence. Weak framing could be said to accompany weak classification. Pedagogic style requires consensus amongst teachers about underlying themes and principles, while the more open frames extend the range of qualities and attributes students are expected to bring to the learning process.

Yet the differences in the integrated codes between the periods of educational restructuring are striking. Classification under vocational coding in fact remains particularly strong, erecting a firm boundary between knowledge and practice and supported by consensual definitions of acceptable transmission. Now, for an increasing proportion of young people the practical, the familiar and immediate, commonsense and every-day knowledge, become the subject of the curriculum, displacing the analytical and cognitive, the unusual and distant, the universal. By constructing a firm boundary between mental and manual knowledge the mode of control implicit in collected codes, of insulation diffusing dangerous knowledge, is retained and reinforced in the coding of vocational curricula. In fact, the framing of such curricula is as strong as under collected codes because there is no shift of power, as Bernstein anticipated, from teachers to students. Rather than working out from the needs of individual young people, the teaching process continues to be based on the transmission of an equally rigid framework of learning. Moreover, the close monitoring of character and performance through detailed profiling becomes not an unintended consequence, but the explicit purpose of evaluation and certification.

Thus although integrated codes of the 1980s involve a change, for an increasing number, in what is to count as having knowledge, there is no change as Bernstein suggested in the structure and distribution of power: in fact, there is an intensification of the existing power structure which is operating to tighten the bonds of socialization and control. As Bernstein could hardly have anticipated, the integrated codes of vocationalism are reintroducing the 'deep closure of (Durkheim's) mechanical solidarity': a homogeneous world of low individuation in which people are assigned to their social roles and held together by common ties and rigid codes of conduct and sentiment. How are we to account for such developments?

EXPLAINING THE RESTRUCTURING OF THE 17+ CURRICULUM

I have described the protracted development, competitively negotiated between the schools and further education sectors, of a vocational curriculum at 17. Bernstein's 1971 paper has provided the means of conceptually mapping those changes, but not of explaining them. How are we to account for the development and assertion of the new vocational code with its distinctive implications for educational socialization and control? I shall examine two theoretical frameworks that are particularly appropriate to an explanatory account of the struggles to implement a new curriculum at 17.

The first theory is based on the concepts of interest, exchange and power. This theory conceives of government as forming a complex network of institutions, organizations, agencies and interest groups. These 'actors' live in an environment of uncertainty produced by the scarcity of resources necessary to ensure survival. They can pursue their interests and acquire the strategic resources necessary for managing uncertainty only by escaping or creating dependencies amongst other actors. Autonomy and power then provide the critical bargaining levers to manipulate exchange relationships in the network. Powerful actors can win more resources and so ensure the delivery of services, implement their policies, as well as protect and extend the boundaries of their influence and domination.

This model, and the strategies which derive from it, seem to be highly appropriate to illuminate the prolonged transactions over the new proposals for a 17+ curriculum.

Governments since the mid-1970s have defined the 17+ as critical to their plans to introduce a more vocationalized curriculum for the 14–19 age group, but lacking the instruments of control possessed by more centralized systems have had to rely on exchange and to deploy what resources they have had accordingly.

In this context the DES has sought to deploy its strategic resources to achieve maximum leverage in bargaining. Control of financial resources is gradually being concentrated at the centre to reduce the discretion of the schools sector, while the limited grants available to the independent bodies, boards and institutes have been manipulated to provide appropriate curricular developments. Monopoly power over the rules of the game has been used to shape circulars and official papers as well as to refuse legal recognition to the CEE. Not only have the official committees and their composition been determined and their agendas defined, but where possible constitutional rights have been activated to facilitate appointments—'this is one of our main influences and controls: where we can appoint a chairman and his council we take the opportunity when necessary.'[14] Controls over finance and the rules of the game change the structure of exchange and the possibility of reciprocation. Coercive sanctions have been applied to undermine the Schools Council or to exclude the CSE exam boards, or to manoeuvre control within the DES branches to limit access and influence to sources of political power. Perhaps the centre's most subtle and pervasive resource is the capacity to articulate and promote new educational ideologies, to lend authority to new integrated codes which underwrite the message systems of curricula, pedagogy and evaluation.

The schools sector has resisted the encroachment upon its territory implied by the state's support for a vocationally oriented exam at 17. Alliances have been mobilized within the DES and amongst ministers to ensure that bargaining over the 17+ proposals reflects concessions to the sometimes traditional collection code interests of schools and teachers. A few sanctions may have been displayed to reinforce the assertion of their position. But although compromises have been achieved, the bargaining position of the schools sector has been particularly weak and vulnerable: the resources available have been limited and they have lacked support at the centre of government whose new ideologies have rendered the powerful indifferent to the skills and resources which schools have to offer. Dependence upon external resources and commitment to skills and values which lack general currency has undermined the interests and influence of the schools sector.

The strategies and transactions of the disparate further education actors are also illuminated by the resource dependency model. Their monopoly of vocational expertise, and domination of fee income derived from those markets, has supported the interests of the world of further education in the development of a (integrated code) vocationally oriented certificate of employability. Institutes such as the CGLI have used their considerable legal and financial autonomy to seize the initiative during periods of inertia and thus increase their subsequent bargaining power. The educational ideologies of integrated curricula articulated by FE colleges, associations and institutes have reflected the purposes of those at the centre of power and made the state more sensitive to the demands and potential use of sanctions by FE interests.

Here appears to be a plausible theoretical framework which does much to help us explain complex developments in the 17+ curriculum. The model suggests that those actors who monopolize resources expand their own autonomy and achieve the compliance of others. Yet there have been actors within both the schools and FE sectors who have possessed wealth and autonomy and not acquired concomitant influence. The stress within the model upon resources does not fully account for the unfolding of the story. In particular, those organizations which have enjoyed closer institutional ties with the state, for example, the FEU or the validating bodies TEC and BEC, have grown in influence and impact over their rivals *within* FE as well as in the school sector.

The explanatory power of the resource dependency theory diminishes in effect when one of the actors ineluctably has recourse to monopoly powers to change the rules of the game, to eliminate summarily inconvenient competitors while creating others in its own image, to control resources but also to manipulate the currency and the rate of exchange, and to possess in reserve an array of sanctions.

The state is not one actor among others but dominates the contemporary stage. To grasp fully the state-led restructuring of education at the present time we need to theorize exchange transactions within a broader understanding of social structure and its contextual problems.

THE STATE AND SYSTEM INTEGRATION

With the deepening economic crises of the 1970s, the state, in this and other countries, has become increasingly preoccupied with the need to re-examine the bases of economy-polity-social system relationships in order to clarify and redefine new points of control. Habermas (1976) has argued that such crises create 'steering problems' for the state if it is to maintain control and integration.

Education has been at the centre of the steering crisis and of attempts to introduce new modes of rationality. Education has been central partly because it is one of the largest policy sectors which has also been faced by extensive problems of control and integration. Demographic decline, together with the reduction of resources to the service, have made the management of contraction a priority for central and local government: schools, staffing and courses have had to be reorganized and rationalized (Briault and Smith, 1980; Dennison, 1981; Ranson, 1980; Walsh *et al.*, 1982; Taylor, 1981; Kogan, 1981). Yet the centrality of education to the steering crisis lies, arguably, less at the level of the resourcing and organization of contraction but derives from concerns about the performance of the economy and more deep-seated structural changes affecting economy and society (cf. Bernbaum, 1979; Ranson, 1982; David, 1980; CCCS, 1982). The progressive substitution of capital for labour in the wake of the new technologies is not merely ensuring the final elimination of manual tasks within traditional manufacturing industries but is more fundamentally bringing into question the nature and necessity of work. The repercussions for the social and political order of such changes are profound. The consequences for the service which, finely woven into that social and political fabric, certificates the distribution of manpower to the labour market, as well as the aspirations that are carried into the market, are equally profound.

The state has sought to control and restructure education in order to facilitate and regulate a period of rapid socio-economic change. Thus a senior DES official: 'there is a need especially in the 16–19 area, for a centrally formulated approach to education: we need what the Germans call "instrumentarium" through which Ministers can implement and operate policy.'[15] The DES has sought to steer a number of dimensions of policy—finance, institutions, staffing—but above all curriculum and assessment: 'I see a return to centralization of a different kind with the centre seeking to determine what goes on in institutions: this is a more fundamental centralization than we have seen before'. The strategy of introducing a vocational course and modes of assessment at 17 has been a central dimension of the state's policies to restructure education.

The state's policies for steering the education system, have been guided, I contend, by three underlying presuppositions: vocationalism, rationalization and stratification. Firstly, *vocationalism:* policy-making fastened on the need to prepare young people more adequately for employment. The young would stand better chances of employment if provided with vocational skills and attitudes, while the efficiency of industry and commerce would be expanded concomitantly. More generally, if schooling could be redirected the deep seated antipathy in our culture towards industrialism and the values of science and technology (cf. Nairn, 1977; Weiner, 1981) could be shifted to the benefit of economic effectiveness. The initiatives in association with the DES of the Schools Council, Department of Industry (DOI) and Confederation of British Industry (CBI) to improve the links at secondary level between school and industry have been an important part of the strategy to improve the understanding teachers and pupils have of the wealth producing sector. But as we have seen, the central thrust towards a vocational reorienting of schooling has been in the courses for 16-year-olds beyond the statutory school leaving age: that is, the DES's 17+ initiative, reinforced by MSC's initiatives in YOP and YTS (Youth Training Schemes) for the young unemployed.

Yet the focus seems manifestly to be upon certain courses for 16–19-year-olds and not others. The traditional A-level course has not been the subject of discussion for vocational redirection and has in fact been reinforced as an academic standard by both Labour and Conservative ministers. But, of course, A-level is a vocational preparation for employment of a certain kind. Perhaps young people are being prepared with different skills for different sectors of the restructured labour market. It is here that we need to explore the second underlying policy presupposition of *rationalization.*

The management of contraction necessitates the national reduction of resources to education and thus the need for the service to radically review and rationalize its resource distribution. The duplication of courses for the 16–19 age group and the inefficiencies in the use of resources between schools and colleges suggested that reorganization and rationalization would offer educational as well as financial advantages. Yet it was well understood by policy-makers in the late 1970s that the question of rationalization really presupposed qualitative policy decisions about educational provision. The resource question is in essence an opportunity question about the educational offering which young people should be provided with. It was in this vein that a Treasury official recommended that the ESGE 16–19 Sub-Committee could only resolve the issue of how to rationalize provision by first determining *how much* opportunity, choice and access should be allowed to which groups of young people: first define desirable levels of participation for the whole age group and then the 'separate' 16–19 client groups. The Macfarlane Report (1980) incorporated clear overtones about the need to rationalize educational opportunities: what was offered in the past may now be unreasonable in cost as well as being unsuited to the nation's economic needs. The aspirations of young people must be realistic and rationalized from now on: 'that a range of opportunities is available of a quality that meets the realistic aspirations of young people, parents and society at a cost which the nation judges it right to pay' (p. 13).

Yet the policy of rationalizing opportunities and encouraging realism of aspiration was not left at the level of exhortation. The rules and procedures embodied in the new course development would systematically determine the outcomes desired. Thus the new 17+ course, in whatever its forms (even the redesigned Keohane style CEE), would ensure not only a vocational preparation for those young people taking the courses but, significantly, their subsequent education and training opportunities. Whereas the Schools Council CEE maintained a connection in its certification with those qualifications which could enable access to higher education, both the Keohane and Mansell committees and the government policy statements deliberately sought to eliminate such a connection. The curricular structures would steer students into the vocational routes desired. Underlying such structures was the third policy presupposition of *stratification*.

The means of achieving the limitation of opportunities for young people is being determined through more sharply differentiated curricular experiences. In the past, 16–19 provision was demand-led in the long term and resource-led in the short term; in the future it will be curriculum-led. How much education should be offered is then a matter that is decided 'internally' by the curricular paths which people become locked into. The strategy is first to identify separate 'client groups' who are claimed to possess significant differences in ability, attainment, aptitude and maturity. Such different groups are then defined as possessing alternative 'needs' which clearly require different provision. The age group, it is increasingly argued by the state, should increasingly be classified and differentiated at 16:

> young people should branch out at the age of 16, each according to his or her abilities ... (Macfarlane Report, p. 17).
>
> there will be increasing differentiation of routes at 16; the academic A level route will become more intensively academic and a jolly good thing too. Within each stream there will

be different but intensive provision. There will be some switching of courses—about as much as there was between the secondary moderns and the grammar schools. (DES senior official)

we have been concerned throughout with the need to promote even-handedness of treatment and parity of esteem within 16–19 education (Macfarlane Report, p. 18)

The rationalization of opportunities, together with a vocationalized and classified curriculum, amount to a more overt stratification of young people than we have previously witnessed. The language of tripartite education— parity of esteem between modern, technical and grammar sectors—having been almost eliminated from the secondary sector will reappear in the tertiary sector. Government officials, particularly the Inspectorate, already talk of three client groups (indeed, HMI have identified a team with functional responsibilities for the three sectors); the tertiary modern group will comprise young people on MSC courses, YOP and now YTS, and on the DES 17+ pre-vocational courses; the tertiary technical group will comprise those on the more advanced TEC and BEC courses and now those young people who will be selected into the new MSC-controlled technical stream courses (TVEI); while the tertiary grammar group will comprise those doing A-levels and beginning university courses. The 17+ vocational courses have their own internal forms of differentiation. As one senior HMI put it, 'the "technical", "business" and "general" modules are conceived as selective streams for a hierarchy of ability: having divided the age group into sheep and goats, we will then divide the goats into those with horns and those without horns.'[16]

CONCLUSION

The present transforming of education is thus once more an attempt to adjust the expectations of young people and their sense of place. The changes seem to embody a conception of future society: 'Education often acts as a kind of metaphor of national destinies. It seems to be a particularly appropriate vehicle for talking about the future of society in general' (CCCS, 1978). In the 1960s the images for young people, as well as for society, were of opportunity, horizons, mobility and achievement. In the 1980s those images are replaced by ones of realism, localism, place and ascription.

NOTES

1. Periodization 1955–75 and 1975–.
2. Extracts from the 'Yellow Book' are taken from *The Times Educational Supplement*, 15 October 1976.
3. Interview notes: SSRC Research into Central-Local Relations 1979–82.
4. Ibid.
5. Ibid.
6. Ibid.
7. A report published by Garnett College (1978) *One Year Pre-Employment Courses for Students Aged 16+: a survey in colleges of further education.*

8. Schools Council (1972) Working Paper 45, '16-19 Growth and Response 1. Curricular Bases'.
9. Keohane Report.
10. Mansell Report.
11. DES (1980), *Examinations 16-18: a consultative document* (Green Paper).
12. DES (1982) *17+ A New Qualification*, May.
13. Bernstein (1975), p. 106.
14. Interview notes (see Note 3).
15. Ibid.
16. Ibid.

REFERENCES

Bernbaum, G. (Ed.) (1979) *Schooling in Decline*, Macmillan, London.
Bernstein, B. (1975) *Class, Codes and Control*, Vol. 3, Routledge & Kegan Paul, London.
Briault, E. and Smith, F. (1980) *Falling Rolls in Secondary Schools*, NFER, Windsor.
Centre for Contemporary Cultural Studies (1982) *Unpopular Education: schooling and social democracy since 1944*, Hutchinson, London.
David, M. (1980) *The State, the Family and Education*, Routledge & Kegan Paul, London.
Dennison, W. (1981) *Education in Jeopardy: problems and possibilities of contraction*, Blackwell, Oxford.
Garnett College (1978) *One Year Pre-employment Courses for Students aged 16+: a survey in colleges of further education*, 1978.
Habermas, J. (1976) *Legitimation Crisis*, Heinemann, London.
HMSO (1977) *Education in Schools: a consultative document* (Green Paper), July.
Keohane Report (1979) *Proposals for a Certificate of Extended Education*, HMSO, London.
Kogan, M. (1981) Education in 'Hard Times', in Hood, C. and Wright, M. *Big Government in Hard Times*, Martin Robertson.
Lawton, D. (1980) *The Politics of the School Curriculum*, Routledge & Kegan Paul, London.
Macfarlane Report (1980) *Education for 16-19 Year Olds*, DES, London.
Mansell Report (1979) *A Basis for Choice*, Further Education Unit, June.
Nairn, T. (1977) *The Break-up of Britain*, NLR.
Plowden Report (1967) *Children and Their Primary Schools*, HMSO, London.
Ranson, S. (1980) Education and falling school rolls, in *Local Government Studies*, **6**, 1.
Ranson, S. (1982) *Central-Local Policy Planning in Education*, SSRC, London.
Schools Council (1972a) 16-19 Growth and Response 1, Curricular Bases, Working Paper 45.
Schools Council (1972b) 16-19 Growth and Response 2, Examination Structure, Working Paper 46.
Taylor, W. (1981) Contraction in context, in Simon, B. and Taylor, W. *Education in the Eighties*, Batsford, London.
Walsh, K. *et al.* (1982) *The Management of Teachers: problems of contraction*, INLOGOV.
Weiner, M. (1981) *English Culture and the Decline of the Industrial Spirit 1950-1980*, Cambridge University Press, Cambridge.
Williams, R. (1961) *The Long Revolution*, Pelican, Harmondsworth.

8

Doomsday of a New Dawn? The Prospects for a Common System of Examining at 16+

DESMOND L. NUTTALL

For over 15 years there has been pressure to merge the Ordinary level of the General Certificate of Education (GCE O-level) and the Certificate of Secondary Education (CSE) into a common system of examining at 16+[1]. The aim of this paper is to examine the aims and motives of those seeking the reform, and of the Department of Education and Science (DES) in reacting to their proposals. The principal thesis that I seek to establish is that the DES has seized upon the occasion of examination reform to make changes to the structure and control of examinations that have no special link to the notion of a common system. This paper also evaluates the prospects for a common system of examining at 16+ as they appear in early 1983.

THE ROOTS OF THE 16+ PROPOSALS

The first set of CSE examinations had barely been taken nationwide before the problems of having two separate examination systems began to emerge. The Joint GCE/CSE Committee of the Schools Council, for example, recommended in 1966 that 'the problem and the nature of the existing situation point towards the development of a common system of grades . . .'.[2]

The potentially divisive effect of having more than one system of examinations was recognized much earlier by the far-sighted Norwood Committee who feared that the School Certificate (established in 1917), being taken in only one type of school, might 'mark off the secondary

Source: From Broadfoot, P. (ed.) (1984) *Selection, Certification and Control*, Falmer Press, Falmer.

grammar school from other forms of secondary education. A system will then become established under which parity in secondary education will become impossible. . . . '[3] Reporting in 1943, they recommended the replacement of the grouped School Certificate by a single-subject examination but only for a transitional period of seven years; after that 'in the interest of the individual child and of the increased freedom and responsibility of the teaching profession, change . . . should be in the direction of making the examination entirely internal, that is to say, conducted by the teachers at the school on syllabuses and papers framed by themselves . . . '.[4]

The single-subject examination duly came into being in 1951 in the form of GCE O-level, but the next stage of a wholly internal examination envisaged by the Norwood Committee has yet to come. Moreover, the examination was designed for, and remained the preserve of, the grammar schools. Predictably there was very soon pressure from the secondary modern schools to be included in the public examination system. In 1955 the then Minister of Education rejected the suggestion that the standard of an O-level pass should be lowered so as to bring the examination within the reach of more pupils.[5] He also stated that he did not favour the establishment of any new general examinations of national standing for secondary schools, but encouraged groups of schools to experiment in organizing their own examinations. Many did so, while others entered fourth-year pupils for examinations organized by national or regional bodies like the Royal Society of Arts or the Union of Lancashire and Cheshire Institutes; the increasing number of those who stayed on into the fifth year beyond the statutory school-leaving age tended to be entered for O-level.[6]

Growth in the demand for external examinations during the 1950s could not be stemmed, and by 1960 the Crowther Committee and the Beloe Committee had both recommended the establishment of an examination for pupils of lower ability than those who would be entered for GCE.[7] The final shape of the new CSE examination proposed by the Secondary School Examinations Council (SSEC) and approved by the DES in 1962 was somewhat different from that proposed by the Beloe Committee in 1960, in particular, the top grade was linked to the standard for an O-level pass in an attempt to help the new examination gain national currency and respect.

THE DEVELOPMENT OF THE PROPOSALS

While national bodies were creating two separate examinations with an eye on the two principal kinds of secondary school—grammar and modern—a much more important movement was gathering momentum: comprehensive schools were slowly being established. There is irony in the fact that it was the same year—1965—that saw both the first CSE examinations in some parts of the country and the issue of DES Circular 10/65 which encouraged the move towards comprehensive reorganization. It is not surprizing, then, that it was only a short time before the Schools Council (which had inherited the examination responsibilities of the SSEC in 1964) began to point out the problems created by the dual system. At this early stage, most concern was expressed about the confusion created in the minds of the public by the existence of a pass/fail classification at O-level and a graded system in CSE that were linked through CSE grade 1, but the organizational, curricular and administrative problems (all of which are considered in more detail below) did not pass unnoticed.

Nevertheless, the CSE introduced many positive features into English public examination practice. CSE examinations employed a much wider range of techniques of examining and assessing than had been the norm in GCE and hence brought a wider range of skills and abilities into the net of assessment; in particular, the participation of the candidate's own teacher in the process of assessment became common along the lines of the Norwood Committee's recommendation. This participation was at its greatest in Mode 3 examinations, where the department or even the individual teacher devised the syllabus and scheme of examination and carried out the assessment, subject only to moderation by the CSE board. The criteria which a Mode 3 proposal was obliged to meet were straightforward and liberal: the subject had to be capable of being examined and moderated, and the title had to provide a correct description of the content.[8] Few proposals failed to meet the first criterion of being capable of being examined and moderated (even in landlocked Middlesex one could find a moderator for Navigation and Seamanship); but for many years most boards took the view that physical education could not be examined, moderated and graded in a manner comparable to other subjects and this criterion was therefore used to reject Mode 3 PE proposals. The second criterion—precise titling—was designed to help users and to stop their being misled; for example, a syllabus consisting exclusively of arithmetic could be titled 'Arithmetic' but not 'Mathematics'. But what of a syllabus that was mainly arithmetic with a sprinkling of other kinds of mathematics? Titles such as 'Arithmetic with Basic Mathematics' had to be invented. Each subject area created similar problems. The result was a proliferation of different titles, a proliferation that was later to be attacked (see below). The only other major control available to a CSE board in respect of Mode 3 was the right to impose a grade ceiling, to rule, say, that no grade higher than 3 could be awarded, if a syllabus did not seem to make comparable demands to similar syllabuses in the same subject.

Until the establishment of the CSE, the GCE system had been subject to some central control. The SSEC had had to approve new syllabuses at both O-level and A-level before a board could introduce them. The Schools Council recognized that the potential number of CSE syllabuses meant that it could not approve each one individually, and it consequently also gave up the practice of approving new O-level syllabuses. For CSE examinations, the Schools Council acted as a court of appeal in the few cases where a board and a school could not reach agreement; for GCE O-level, its powers were negligible though the GCE boards informed the Schools Council if new subjects were to be examined, and the Council sometimes asked to see and comment upon these new syllabuses. At 16+, then, central control or even monitoring of examination syllabuses was relaxed in the 1960s to such an extent that it was virtually non-existent. (At A-level, though, the Schools Council retained the right to approve all new syllabuses.)

It was, however, considerations of politics and philosophy as much as considerations of practicality that led the teacher-controlled Schools Council to allow the CSE boards, also teacher-controlled, more autonomy in the sphere of syllabus approval than the GCE boards had had under the reign of the SSEC. In retrospect, one can see this era of the mid-1960s as the zenith of the period of autonomy of schools and teachers. One of the principal bastions of defence against the further spread of teacher autonomy was the GCE boards, most of which were controlled by the universities in the final analysis, though teachers played a large and increasing part in the determination of policy. One of the motives of some of those arguing for a merging of CSE and O-level, especially the teacher-politicians in the Schools Council, was the desire to remove this obstacle to increased teacher autonomy by importing the typically more democratic methods of the CSE into the realm of the GCE. Others simply wanted to see the wider range of examining methods and opportunities of CSE available in GCE as well.

But these were arguments that seldom reached the surface of the debate within the Schools Council.[9] There, and later more widely, stimulated by Schools Council publications and leaflets,[10] the principal arguments were about the divisiveness of a dual system (as forecast by the Norwood Committee) and about the organizational, curricular and administrative problems that it created. The divisiveness came about from the lack of status accorded by parents and employers to the CSE in comparison to the well-established GCE. The failure of the CSE to gain parity of esteem with the GCE mirrored the failure of the secondary modern to gain parity of esteem with the grammar school. In the eyes of its supporters, comprehensive education required a comprehensive examination system; the effect of a dual system within the comprehensive school was to create grammar and secondary modern streams. Children had to be categorized into GCE and CSE groups, often at the beginning of the fourth year; not only did this categorization fail to match any natural division between the aspirations or abilities of the children, but it also created organizational and timetabling problems. To provide a safety net, many schools entered borderline candidates for both GCE and CSE, putting a severe burden on just those pupils who were having difficulty with the GCE course. And a severe burden, as well as a considerable increase in costs, was placed on the schools who had to cope with at least two different boards, with their different entry dates, stationery and examination timetables.

Aware of all these problems created by the dual system, in July 1970 the Governing Council of the Schools Council resolved, by sixty-four votes to one, 'that there should be a single examination system at the age of 16+ and that this should be under the Schools Council'. A working party was quickly established; it reported in 1971, making a number of firm recommendations about the proposed system (notably that the percentile range 40–100 should be adopted initially as the range of ability to be covered) and indicating areas needing further study, such as the technical problem of examining over a wide range of ability.[11]

Then began one of the largest programmes of feasibility and development studies of a proposed educational innovation ever mounted in England and Wales. Some fifty studies were mounted by consortia of GCE and CSE boards, most involving examinations leading to the award of both GCE and CSE certificates (rather than simply trial papers leading to no qualification). In 1974 these examinations spanned seventeen major areas of the curriculum and about 68,000 subject entries were made. Ironically enough, many of these experimental examinations, albeit slightly modified in the light of experience, continue to this day, most notably in Wales and the north of England, and have recruited hundreds of thousands of entries. At the same time, research into related topics such as the moderation of course work and into Mode 3 was being undertaken by the staff of the Schools Council.[12]

The task of evaluating this programme of work and hence the feasibility of the common system of examining at 16+ fell upon the Joint Examinations Sub-Committee of the Schools Council who delivered their report in the summer of 1975.[13] Their principal conclusions were that the common system was feasible and that the research programme indicated ways in which the outstanding problems could be solved. Given the power of the common system to eliminate the problems of the dual system, they had no hesitation in recommending that a common system should be established as soon as possible. After nearly a year of consultation and public debate about the report, the Governing Council of the Schools Council decided in July 1976 to endorse the recommendations of their sub-committee and forwarded them to the DES, where the decision whether or not to implement them constitutionally rests.

Proposals for a teacher-controlled and fairly liberal new examining system, linked to the ideal of comprehensive education, could not have been sent to the DES at a less auspicious time than the middle of 1976. In the wake of what Halsey dubbed 'the rotting of public confidence in public institutions'[14] and precipitated by the economic effects of the oil crisis of 1973/74, there was growing concern about the responsiveness of the educational system to national needs and the standards of education being provided, especially by comprehensive schools. Elsewhere Bowe and Whitty analyze the forces at work and show how concern about the relevance of the curriculum was later overtaken by concern about the broader issue of standards: in both cases, however, a large part of the blame for the inadequacies of the system was placed upon the teaching profession, whose autonomy should, it was felt, therefore be curbed. The principal issues were the curriculum and teaching methods, and the DES, with the help of HM Inspectorate, were eager to have more influence over these, as the Yellow Book (a confidential memorandum prepared in the DES) made clear. The Yellow Book was part of the briefing for the famous speech made in October 1976 by the then Prime Minister, James Callaghan.[15] He made it clear that the public, as well as the teaching profession, had a right to a say in what goes on in schools, and launched the so-called Great Debate about education. A formal part of this debate was a series of regional conferences early in 1977 at which the agenda covered four main topics: the curriculum; the assessment of standards; the education and training of teachers; school and working life. It is the debate on the curriculum and its consequences that are of particular significance for the proposals for a common system at 16+.

THE CURRICULUM DEBATE

After the regional conferences, the Government published a Green Paper.[16] It identified four points of concern about the curriculum in secondary schools, two of which concerned the problems caused by variations in the curriculum between schools, and the third the lack of match between the curriculum of many schools and life in a modern industrial society. The proposed remedy was some form of core curriculum common to all secondary schools, but the difficulty of creating a suitable core curriculum was acknowledged.

Subsequent events showed how right the Government was to acknowledge the difficulty. Four years of information-gathering and consultation later, the proposals in *The School Curriculum* (issued by the DES in 1981) were bland in the extreme.[17] A leader in *The Times Educational Supplement* had this to say:

> *The School Curriculum* represents the liquidation of commitments to a core curriculum and a defined framework, which Ministers entered into without understanding what was involved. It is not a very glorious retreat, but at least it gets this tiresome business out of the DES's hair and leaves it to the professionals.[18]

THE EXAMINATION DEBATE

Variation in the curriculum from school to school was mirrored in—some might say, fuelled by—the variation in examination syllabuses. The Expenditure Committee (Home Office, Education and the Arts) of the House of Commons stressed the importance of comparability of standards in public examinations and argued for a reduction in the diversity of the content of syllabuses in the same subject.[19] Similar points about unnecessary and harmful diversity were made at many of the regional conferences during the Great Debate; at one, the Secretary to the University of London University Entrance and School Examinations Council (the London GCE Board) proposed that all A-level syllabuses in the same subject should share some common core of content, a proposal that was hailed by the press as one of the more sensible suggestions to emerge from the Great Debate.[20]

Partly as a result of these pressures and partly as a result of the continuing process of syllabus revision at A-level, the GCE boards began to see merit in delineating material that might be common to all syllabuses in a given subject, starting with mathematics. The Standing Conference on University Entrance enthusiastically latched on to this idea, on the grounds that it would ease the task of teaching in the first year of a university course if all students had experienced much the same course in the sixth form, and just beat the GCE boards to the production of a suggested common core for mathematics. Many other subjects have since been covered, and new syllabuses embodying some of the common cores are now in use.

Diversity in syllabus content was not the only charge levelled at public examinations. Burgess and Adams summarized many others: their lack of comprehensiveness in covering all the aims of education, their exclusion of a large minority, their cost and their obtrusiveness into the organization and administration of schools, to name but four.[21] HM Inspectorate, in their survey of secondary schools, roundly criticized the way in which concentration upon examination requirements narrowed learning opportunities in the fourth and fifth years.[22] They felt that the curriculum and examinations had to be brought more closely together, to make examinations a force for good rather than a force for harm. To do this, they argued,

> ... there is a case for the participation of more teachers both in devising syllabuses and in assessing their pupils, particularly in those aspects of work which cannot easily be tested within a timed written examination. The benefits of a balance of board-based and school assessment would apply to all pupils and not merely to the average and less able. The introduction of a new system of examining would afford opportunity as well as reason for the development of more broadly based methods of assessment which match changes in the curriculum.[23]

CONSIDERATION OF THE 16+ PROPOSALS BY THE DES

The DES have reacted slowly and cautiously to the proposals for a common system of examining at 16+, ever since the Schools Council sent them in mid-1976. Their slowness has no doubt been due in part to the changes of government and of ministers, but both their slowness and caution have been influenced by the public debate about the curriculum, examinations and standards. At the same time, there seems to have been a growing realization that, as the Inspectorate point out in the quotation above, the occasion of examination reform provides the ideal opportunity to put right a number of defects in the existing examination system that

> are quite independent of the existence of a dual system of grading. There are too many awarding bodies and too many syllabuses, including an unnecessary number with the same title: and different titles which sometimes conceal only marginal differences in the scope of syllabuses. Moreover, the relationship between overlapping grades needs to be properly established. Since examination requirements in many subjects are not clear, schools can interpret them in a way which is harmful to good education. The performance expected of candidates needs to be clearly described and the standards for each grade need to be made more explicit.[24]

As the Government now see it, the way to remedy these defects is through the development of national criteria; the history of these national criteria in the development of the 16+ proposals shows how they have emerged from almost nowhere in 1976 to be the key factor in determining the future of the 16+ proposals.

THE NATIONAL CRITERIA

The criteria governing the acceptance or rejection of a Mode 3 submission have been described above and are considered by Bowe and Whitty, who also point to the very much more stringent criteria applied to Mode 3 submissions by the GCE boards.[25] This difference in practice led the Schools Council to note that 'consideration would have to be given, in the development stage of a new examination, to the criteria by which [Mode 2, and Mode 3 and mixed-mode] schemes might be accepted.'[26] This was the only reference to criteria in the 16+ proposals, though the criteria to be applied by boards to Mode 3 submissions in the proposed Certificate of Extended Education were debated fully in the Schools Council and spelt out in some detail in the proposals that also went to the DES in 1976.

The response of Shirley Williams, at that time Secretary of State for Education and Science, to the Schools Council's 16+ proposals came within a week of Callaghan's famous speech at Ruskin College, and was cautious in the extreme. Ignoring the defects of the existing examinations seized upon by her successors in office, she wrote: 'I believe that the public has confidence in the standards of the existing examinations and their consistency across the country. This confidence is too valuable to be put at risk.'[27] She announced that she felt it necessary to institute a further 'intensive and systematic study' of the proposals and the evidence that supported them.

This study was carried out by a committee composed of nominated persons from inside and outside the world of education, including HMIs and civil servants, under the chairmanship of Sir James Waddell (himself a retired civil servant). Inevitably, it went over exactly the same ground as the Schools Council had, but could draw on two more years' experience of the experimental 16+ examinations and had more staff and resources at its disposal. Nevertheless, the Committee reached essentially the same conclusions as the Schools Council, in particular that a common system of examining was feasible. But it was critical of the trial examinations in many subjects, because they had employed examination papers (or other assessment devices) taken by all candidates in common. These, the Committee (and many others) felt, could not do justice to candidates at the extremes of the ability range. The Committee therefore recommended much more extensive use of alternative papers at different levels of difficulty (what they termed 'differentiated papers') so that more able candidates could follow a harder route and less able candidates an easier one but without access to the award of the top grades. They also recommended much stronger coordination of the examination system than had been seen in the past, with nationally agreed criteria as the key ingredient.[28]

The Government accepted the conclusions and recommendations of the Waddell Committee. In a White Paper published in October 1978, they announced that

> ... publicly known general criteria should be established to ensure that syllabuses in subjects important for subsequent stages of education or of vocational relevance have sufficient in common, and are relevant to the needs of subsequent courses of education and employment, to enable the grades awarded to be accepted with confidence by those concerned.

They also required criteria specific to each major subject, and expected the national criteria 'to ensure that alternative papers are used wherever this is necessary to maintain standards.'[30]

The change in government in May 1979 caused a pause in the consideration and refinement of the 16+ proposals. The new Conservative Government were more receptive to the lobbying of the GCE boards, whose initiative in establishing common cores at A-level had surely not gone unnoticed and whose role in maintaining standards and in resisting teacher control was widely recognized. So in February 1980 when Mark Carlisle, the new Secretary of State for Education and Science, announced that the Government would continue with the plans to establish a common system, it was no surprise that, in addition to reaffirming support for national criteria and differentiated papers, he gave the GCE boards a special accolade. In a DES Press Notice Carlisle observed:

> Any reforms must ensure that the high standards associated with GCE O-level are maintained. This must be our first priority. We intend to make the GCE boards responsible for the higher grades in the new scale.[31]

He also indicated that schools would still be free to choose among the examinations offered by the various groups of collaborating GCE and CSE boards. This principle of freedom of choice of board reflects existing practice in the GCE system (in contrast to the practice in the CSE system where the freedom of choice is between modes of examination within a board, and not between the syllabuses of different boards); the principle is also held very dear by the GCE boards.

The GCE and CSE boards then jointly embarked upon the preparation of criteria at the invitation of the DES, though they were given relatively little guidance: 'The exact nature and scope of the criteria are difficult to predict at this stage. It may not be possible to be precise until a good deal of further work has been done.'[32] It was thus left to the GCE and CSE boards to clarify the nature of the criteria, which they decided should cover aims, assessment objectives, content, techniques of assessment and grade descriptions for Grade 3 (equivalent to O-level Grade C) and Grade 6 (CSE Grade 4). During 1982, the draft criteria for some twenty subjects were published, in many cases receiving extensive criticism, and revised draft criteria were submitted to yet another new Secretary of State, Sir Keith Joseph, early in 1983.

One of the most criticized acts of Sir Keith Joseph has been the abolition of the Schools Council, announced in Summer 1982, and its replacement by a proposed School Curriculum Development Council and the Secondary Examinations Council, which started work in April 1983. The Secondary Examinations Council consists of the nominees of the secretary of state (admittedly largely picked from names offered by a wide range of educational bodies), rather than democratically appointed representatives of different interests as in the Schools Council; more significantly, fewer than one-quarter of its members are practising teachers so that any possibility of teacher domination has been clearly eliminated from the central controlling mechanism for the public examination system. The first task of the Secondary Examinations Council is to appraise the revised draft national criteria and to advise the Secretary of State (with whom rests the final decision) as to whether these criteria provide a satisfactory basis for the implementation of a common system of examining at 16+.

The aims and nature of the national criteria are spelt out in a DES policy statement issued in November 1982. In most respects they follow the previous DES policy statements discussed above, but more detail is given and more implications are spelt out. For example, the diversity of syllabuses under Mode 3 that has allowed important curriculum development, not least response to the calls for relevance to industry and commerce, will be drastically curtailed; although all modes of examining will be permitted under the new system, the proviso is that the syllabuses and schemes of assessment comply with the national criteria. Moreover, there will be criteria for the inclusion of a subject in the list of those available for examination, implying that any new subject (the 1980s equivalent of computer studies, perhaps) may have a long battle before it can be admitted to the ranks of the 'examinable'. More positively, the DES

will be looking for criteria which reflect the best of current curriculum practice and reinforce an approach to the secondary school curriculum which recognizes the practical application of academic skills: and which are sufficiently flexible to allow new developments to take place.[33]

These requirements will no doubt warm the hearts of HM Inspectorate: Sheila Browne, the Senior Chief Inspector, feels that '... the exercise to establish criteria for the common exam system at 16-plus offers yet another chance—perhaps the last this century—to embody in the exam system aims long aspired to.'[34]

But can the national criteria achieve such a laudable goal? The Inspectorate (as evidenced by their collective view quoted above) feel that participation by more teachers in the processes of syllabus development and the assessment of their own pupils, coupled with the development of more broadly based methods of assessment, are important steps towards this goal. At the present time, the draft national criteria have failed to inspire confidence on these points; in particular, they have consistently revealed a distaste for school-based assessment, which arguably provides the only real way of widening the range of assessment objectives. By giving the GCE boards a right of veto, the DES have ensured that this distaste will be perpetuated in the common system. By requiring Mode 3 proposals to meet the national criteria, the DES have closed off an important avenue of curriculum development and experimentation (and may have blocked a vital professional safety valve), and made it likely that fewer teachers rather than more will be involved in syllabus development and assessment.

CONCLUSIONS

If the opportunity for much needed reforms as perceived by HM Inspectorate has been largely lost in the very slow movement towards a common system of examining at 16+, what of the original advantages seen in the late 1960s—the elimination of divisiveness, greater curricular and organizational flexibility, and simpler administration?

Few of these advantages now seem likely to be present in a common system. By insisting on differentiated assessment in most if not all subjects, the DES have perpetuated the need to select pupils for different courses at about the age of 13 or 14 (though possibly somewhat later than under the dual system), with all that this selection implies in terms of a differentiated curriculum and class organization in the fourth and fifth years. Moreover, by limiting the target group for the design of the examination to the top 60 per cent of pupils in each subject another sort of divisiveness (between the examined and the non-examinable) would become more obvious than it is at present and further curricular complexity would be introduced into the comprehensive school.[35]

By allowing schools a choice of board and groups of boards (and exhorting LEAs not to restrict this freedom of choice[36]), the DES have failed to maximize the chances of administrative streamlining. There may be a common examination timetable nationwide, thus eliminating the possibility of a candidate entering the same subject in more than one board, but there will be different sets of entry forms, stationery requirements and regulations for schools to cope with.

Above all, the incredibly slow pace of the reform and the fact that those with the greatest vested interest—the boards themselves—have been given the task of doing all the drafting make it unlikely that the new system will adequately meet today's curricular needs in which the education and training of those over 16 has taken on a new significance and will head in new directions. Assessment as a teaching and counselling device through the medium of profiles has become the norm for 17-year-olds on vocational preparation courses in further education,[37] and both profiles and graded tests are spreading rapidly in secondary education in an effort to counter the divisive effect of the current public examination system and the feared greater divisiveness of the proposed common system.[38] The inevitable problems of negotiating changes to the national criteria once established make the likely pace of any future development needed to meet changing educational and societal needs so ponderously slow that an analogy between the common system and a dinosaur, and their respective evolutions, is compelling.

In short, there is every danger that the common system now being created will be divisive, bureaucratic, retrogressive and obsolescent—almost exactly the opposite of the common system as desired by its proponents of the late 1960s and early 1970s.

But some features of a common system could be very different. The DES have taken upon themselves a much more overt role in steering examination reforms and giving themselves rights (unprecedented since 1945) over the approval of the detailed content of examination syllabuses and schemes of examination, since it is the DES that have the final say over the national criteria. Having failed in their attempts to control or influence markedly the curriculum through documents like *A Framework for the School Curriculum*,[39] they can succeed by another route, at least for the curriculum of secondary schools.

In practice, this seizing back of control by the DES will have three main effects. First, the number of syllabuses and subjects for which examinations will be available will be drastically curtailed, and the professional autonomy of schools and teachers to design a secondary school curriculum to meet the needs of their pupils correspondingly reduced. Second, the autonomy of the examination boards is similarly being reduced and, as is true more broadly in the sphere of local government, local and regional powers of decision-making are fading away while the powers of central government and institutions grow. This centralization of control is designed, in part at least, to curb the autonomy of teachers in their schools and classrooms, and collectively in the examination boards. The third effect is even more obviously to limit teacher influence at the centre; by replacing the democratic Schools Council, with its responsibilities for coordinating the public examination system and advising the DES on policy, by a Secondary Examinations Council with members nominated by the Secretary of State and with teacher-members in a small minority, teacher influence on examinations policy and practice has been cut back at all levels of the educational decision-making process.

The terms on which a common system might be introduced have been made increasingly stringent by the DES ever since 1976; the judges of the criteria are the DES, acting on the advice of the Secondary Examinations Council, with Sir Keith Joseph and Dr Rhodes Boyson as the final arbiters. The criteria for judging the national criteria were clarified in 1982:

> The national criteria will need to do justice to all pupils in the range of ability for which GCE and CSE examinations are designed, and to set standards at least equal to those of existing examinations at 16+. The syllabuses and forms of assessment adopted must be seen to promote good educational practice and give schools and pupils an incentive to demonstrate their attainments. The arrangements must be intelligible to parents and employers and demonstrably more efficient in the use of resources than the present arrangement.[40]

But the DES have also realized that their particular goals (reducing curriculum diversity and curbing teacher autonomy) could be achieved within the existing system, that is, without the need for introducing a common system of examining at 16+. If the national criteria do not 'fully satisfy' the DES, they would wish to see 'how the national criteria, as by then developed, might best be used to harmonize and improve the dual system.'[41] The threat is quite clear: if the boards do not or cannot create the system the DES want to see, the existing systems will continue with virtually none of the advantages originally hoped for in a common system and with major restrictions placed upon existing practice in syllabus design and assessment methods. A step towards a comprehensive examination for the comprehensive school, as the common system of examining was perceived by many, will be bought at a very heavy price, if indeed it can be bought at all. And the price of an abortive purchase will be even higher.

NOTES

1. *Examinations at 16-plus: a statement of policy,* DES/Welsh Office, November 1982.
2. *Examining at 16+.* The Report of the Joint GCE/CSE Committee of the Schools Council, HMSO, 1966, p. 5. (Although the first CSE examinations were held in some parts of the country in 1965, it was not until summer 1966 that all fourteen CSE boards held examinations.)
3. *Curriculum and Examinations in Secondary Schools,* Report of the SSEC appointed by the President of the Board of Education (the Norwood Report), HMSO, 1943 (reprinted, 1962), p. 46. The School Certificate was the major matriculation requirement of the universities, and to gain the Certificate or the Higher Certificate it was necessary to satisfy the examiners simultaneously in a specified number and range of subjects (an arrangement commonly called a grouped certificate). Only a very small proportion of school leavers, exclusively from grammar and independent schools, gained the Certificate.
4. Ibid., p. 140.
5. Circular 289, Ministry of Education, 1955.

6. This use of O-level in secondary modern schools exacerbated the tendency for the curriculum of the secondary modern to ape that of the grammar school, and its failure to develop a distinctive approach.

7. *15 to 18.* A Report of the Central Advisory Council for Education (England) (the Crowther Report), HMSO, 1959; *Secondary School Examinations Other than the GCE,* Report of a Committee appointed by the SSEC (the Beloe Report), HMSO, 1960. For a more detailed account of the history of examinations see Montgomery, R.J. (1965) *Examinations: an account of their evolution as administrative devices,* Longmans Green.

8. Memorandum to Examining Boards No. 13 issued by the SSEC, c. 1963.

9. For details of the debate within the Schools Council, see *Examinations at 16+: proposals for the future,* The Report of the Joint Examinations Sub-committee of the Schools Council on a common system of examining at 16+, with an evaluation, conclusions and recommendations, Schools Council, 1975.

10. *Arguments for a Common System of Examining at 16+,* Schools Council leaflet, 1973 and ibid.

11. *A Common System of Examining at 16+,* Schools Council Examinations Bulletin 23, Evans/Methuen Educational, 1971.

12. This research programme and its findings are summarized in *Examinations at 16+: proposals for the future.* The principal studies were reported in full in Schools Council Examinations Bulletins 34 and 37.

13. *Examinations at 16+: proposals for the future,* op. cit.

14. Paper given by A.H. Halsey at an SSRC Seminar on Aspects of Accountability, 11 September 1979.

15. The speech is reported in *The Times Educational Supplement,* 22 October 1976. For a fuller account of the events leading up to and following from Mr Callaghan's Ruskin Speech see, for example, *Accountability and Evaluation,* Block I of Course E364, *Curriculum Evaluation and Assessment in Educational Institutions,* The Open University Press, 1982.

16. *Education in Schools: a consultative document* (the Green Paper), HMSO, 1977 (Cmnd 6869), p. 11.

17. *The School Curriculum,* HMSO, 1981.

18. *The Times Educational Supplement,* 27 March 1981, p. 2.

19. Tenth Report from the Expenditure Committee, *Attainments of the School Leaver,* HMSO, 1977.

20. A.R. Stephenson, personal communication.

21. Burgess, T. and Adams, E. (eds.) (1980) *Outcomes of Education,* Macmillan Education.

22. *Aspects of Secondary Education in England: a survey by HM Inspectorate of Schools,* HMSO, 1979.

23. Ibid., p. 244.

24. *Examinations at 16+: a statement of policy,* op. cit., para. 3.

25. Bowe, R. and Whitty, G. 'Teachers, Boards and Standards: the attack on school based assessment in English public examinations at 16+', in Broadfoot, P. (ed.) *Selection, Certification and Control,* Falmer, 1984.

26. *Examinations at 16+: proposals for the future,* op. cit., p. 61.

27. Letter from Mrs Shirley Williams to Sir Alex Smith, Chairman of the Schools Council, 25 October 1976.

28. *School Examinations,* Report of the Steering Committee established to consider proposals for replacing the General Certificate of Education Ordinary-level and Certificate of Secondary Education examinations by a common system of examining (the Waddell Report), HMSO, 1978 (Cmnd 7281).

29. *Secondary School Examinations: a single system at 16 plus* (the White Paper), HMSO, 1978 (Cmnd 7368), p. 10.

30. Ibid., p. 11.

31. *Single Sixteen Plus Exam System,* DES Press Notice, 19 February 1980.

32. Letter from P.H. Halsey (Under-Secretary at DES) to the Secretary of the Standing Conference of Regional Boards, 28 February 1980.

33. *Examinations at 16+: a statement of policy,* op. cit., para. 22.

34. Reported in *Education,* 30 October 1981, p. 340.

35. The existing CSE and O-level systems are jointly designed, officially at least, for the top 60 per cent of the ability range in each subject, but in practice well over 80 per cent of 16-year-

olds take examinations in English and a mathematical subject and more than 90 per cent take at least one public examination. So that under a new system, with a rigidly enforced target group policed by national criteria, a substantially larger proportion of 16-year-olds could expect to be 'unexaminable'.

36. *Examinations at 16+: a statement of policy*, op. cit., para. 14(ix).
37. For a variety of examples see *Profiles*, Further Education Unit, 1982.
38. See, for example, Harrison, A. (1982) *A Review of Graded Tests*, Schools Council Examinations Bulletin 41, Methuen Educational, Balogh, J. (1982) *Profile Reports for School Leavers* Longman; and Goacher, B. (1983) *Recording Achievement at 16+*, Longman.
39. HMSO, 1980.
40. *Examinations at 16+: a statement of policy*, op. cit., para. 4.
41. Ibid., para. 32.

9

A Critique of the APU

CAROLINE GIPPS

Following a seminar on accountability and education held at Cambridge in September 1977, the Social Science Research Council (now the Economic and Social Research Council) set aside a sum of money for research on accountability. Slightly less than half the funds were awarded to a team at the Institute of Education to carry out a three-year project, one of the main tasks of which was to evaluate the work of the Assessment of Performance Unit (APU). The other task was to investigate the extent and impact of LEA testing programmes. In carrying out the research the team interviewed LEA advisers, heads and teachers, both about LEA testing and about the impact of the APU's work. We reported on the LEA testing at the end of 1983.[1]

This article is based on our report on the APU.[2] In writing the report we had access to APU committee papers and minutes as well as APU personnel, and we are indebted to the DES/APU for their co-operation. Like others, we had access to all the published material on the APU—publicity material, reports, etc.—but we did not have access to test items. Nor were we given access to any information on schools or LEAs involved in the APU's testing programme since this was confidential information. As well as reading minutes and documents we interviewed over 40 people involved at some time or another with the APU. This interview material was invaluable in shaping our understanding of the history of the Unit and in clarifying the problem facing those whose job it was to make decisions about the paths along which the APU was to go.

For readers who are not familiar with the APU, we start with a brief description, incorporating some of its history. We then bring the history up to date and give our evaluation of the APU's work.

Source: From Nuttall, D. (ed.) (1985) *Assessing Educational Achievements*, Falmer Press, Falmer.

WHAT IS THE APU?[3]

The APU is a unit within the Department of Education and Science. It is headed by a senior HMI, the professional head, and a senior civil servant, the administrative head. They report to an Under-Secretary and ultimately to the Permanent Secretary at the DES. The Unit oversees the surveying of performance in maths and language at 11 and 15, science at 11, 13 and 15 and first modern foreign language at 13. The Unit is also considering the possibility of monitoring design and technology, and a decision is expected on this in the spring (1984). Given the emphasis on practical skills in Sir Keith Joseph's Sheffield speech[4] a topic such as design and technology would be high on the agenda for monitoring, but the cost of the exercise might militate against it. Aesthetic and physical development were also considered for monitoring; it has now been decided that these are not suitable for national assessment, but the discussion documents produced by the exploratory groups are available for use by LEAs. Plans to assess two highly contentious areas, personal and social development and the performance of West Indian children, have also been dropped. These decisions were taken as a result of widespread consultation both within and without the APU committee structure.

The actual test development and surveying is contracted out to the National Foundation for Educational Research (NFER) for maths, language and modern language and to Leeds University/Chelsea College, London, for science. Each of the development teams has a steering group to advise them, and these groups are composed of teachers, advisers, researchers, lecturers and HMI, all of whom are nominated by the DES. All the steering groups are chaired by HMI attached to the APU. There is also a Statistics Advisory Group made up of DES, NFER and outside statisticians and researchers, which advises the Unit on the technical aspects of its work.

Over all these groups and teams sits the Consultative Committee with approximately thirty members, of whom about two-thirds are appointed by teacher and LEA associations or represent parents, industry and research. The other members, drawn from the HMI and DES, are nominees of the Secretary of State while the chairman is an academic. Thus the Consultative Committee is the only group representative of outside interests. Its role was defined in an early APU publicity leaflet as one of examining the broad outlines and priorities that are proposed for the Unit's work and bringing its influence to bear on them.[5].

There also used to be a Coordinating Group which, as its name implies, coordinated the work of the various groups and reported to the Consultative Committee rather as an executive would. Of the seventeen members, ten were HMI or DES personnel and one was from the NFER, while the remaining six were chosen by the DES from schools, colleges, universities and LEAs. This group was disbanded in early 1980.

HOW THE APU BEGAN

To understand the APU fully, it is necessary to go back over 15 years and look at the APU's precursors.

In the late 1960s several strands came together which were to encourage, within the DES, an interest in national monitoring. First, there was growing interest in subjecting the education system to systematic study of its objectives and evaluation of its achievements. At the same time, there was increasing discussion about trends in educational standards. Critics of the reorganization of secondary education were claiming that standards would fall[6] and there was also concern about 'underachievement' of particular groups, especially ethnic minorities. The NFER had carried out a series of reading surveys from 1948 to 1964 which showed steadily improving performance but there was little information in other areas, especially mathematics. Finally, there seems to have been an increasing concern around 1970 that the DES (as distinct from HMI) was excluded from involvement with the educational curriculum, despite funding the system and ultimately being held accountable for it. Since the Schools Council and the teachers themselves retained control over the curriculum, DES involvement with testing presented itself as a means of obtaining direct evaluation of the performance of the system and consequently a means of achieving some say in curriculum content.

All these strands came together in 1970 with the setting up under the DES planning branch of a working group on the measurement of educational attainment (WGMET).[7] It consisted of two administrators, two HMIs and four academics. The working group reported at the end of 1971 and its main conclusions were that 'regular measurements of educational attainment are desirable', that 'measurement is feasible', should 'be done by sampling' covering 'the main educational stages and school subjects' and should be 'a partnership between testing bodies, the Schools Council, LEAs and the DES'. The group recommended an early start, and arising from this, a feasibility project at the NFER (Tests of Attainment in Mathematics in Schools) was commissioned by the newly formed DES Policy Group B in 1972. This project became the precursor to the APU maths monitoring programme. In 1974 an interim report from the project indicated that large-scale maths monitoring was clearly feasible and could be undertaken by the NFER.

Also in 1972 the committee of enquiry into reading and the use of English, the Bullock Committee, was set up. This had a monitoring sub-committee which included two administrators, one HMI, two NFER representatives and four educationists and academics. The outcome of the discussions of this sub-committee formed Chapter 3 of the Bullock Committee report.[8] The recommendations went much further than the 1970 group's report and strongly recommended a national system of monitoring, using 'light sampling' and item banking techniques, both of which it was felt could overcome 'curriculum backwash' problems. The report attached great importance to a monitoring system which could make statements about trends in performance.

Thus by the end of 1974, when the APU was formally announced, there had been a strong series of recommendations in favour of national monitoring in the areas of maths and reading.

The intimation that the APU was on its way came in April 1974 in a speech by the then Secretary of State for Education, Mr Reg Prentice, to the National Association of Schoolmasters' Conference.[9] In August of the same year came the first official announcement in the White Paper *Educational Disadvantage and the Educational Needs of Immigrants*.[10] This paper announced the setting up of an Educational Disadvantage Unit (EDU) within the DES, the purpose of which was to influence the allocation of resources in the interests of those suffering from educational disadvantage which, given the focus of the White Paper, was generally understood to mean ethnic minority groups. The EDU was to develop, *in conjunction with the APU*, criteria to improve identification of this educational disadvantage. It was in an annex to this paper that the APU's terms of reference and tasks were set out formally for the first time.

The Unit's terms of reference are:

> To promote the development of methods of assessing and monitoring the achievement of children at school, and to seek to identify the incidence of under-achievement.

The tasks laid down are:

(1) To identify and appraise existing instruments and methods of assessment which may be relevant for these purposes.

(2) To sponsor the creation of new instruments and techniques for assessment, having due regard to statistical and sampling methods.

(3) To promote the conduct of assessment in cooperation with local education authorities and teachers.

(4) To identify significant differences of achievement related to the circumstances in which children learn, including the incidence of underachievement, and to make findings available to those concerned with resource allocation within government departments, local education authorities and schools.

However, publicity material produced by the APU between 1977 and 1980 carried quite a different message: the APU's role was to monitor in order to provide information on standards and how these change over time. There was no mention of underachievement, the circumstances in which children learn, or resource allocation.

Clearly, both from its early publicity material and from the way it has approached its task, as well as its pre-history, the APU's main aim was to monitor standards. Why then was it announced in the way that it was:

'disguised' by a concern about the educational disadvantage of ethnic minority groups? Both the Great Debate, which started in 1976 when Callaghan gave his Ruskin College speech, and the accountability movement which also sprang up in the mid-1970s, were a culmination of an increasingly questioning attitude in the early seventies among commentators, and sections of the general public too, towards the outcomes of the maintained education system. Thus, given the climate at the time when the APU was announced, any proposal to monitor standards nationally would have been strongly resisted by the teaching profession which was feeling under attack. However, assessing the needs of disadvantaged children is less questionable professionally and so the announcement of the APU, presented as part of a programme for dealing with disadvantage and underachievement, created little dissent among educationists.

Why then did dissent appear later? What led up to the publication in 1979 and 1980 of several articles criticizing the APU and its likely effects? These are interesting questions for, as sociologists like Broadfoot[11] have argued, in the past the *efficiency* of assessment has been the main area of concern, not its purpose and effects. With the advent of the APU, however, this has changed, for the criticisms have centred on its wider effect although the efficiency of the programme has been questioned too.

The first reason is that by 1975 it had become clear that the APU was not assessing underachievement and disadvantage as originally announced, but was going to become a full-scale national assessment programme concerned with standards. Why was a national assessment programme considered to be dangerous? Though few observers believed that the more extreme aspects of the American accountability-through-testing model—such as basing teacher dismissals or school closures on test scores—would come into play in this country, when the APU showed that it aimed to monitor standards there was some concern that the APU was intended as an instrument to force accountability on schools and therefore teachers. Though ostensibly concerned with children's standards, this was interpreted as dealing with teachers' competencies. However, by adhering to the principle of light sampling the APU has gone a long way towards allaying fears over its intentions. Also, because only a small number of children is tested at any time and the names of children are not known to researchers, there is no way in which results can be used to judge individual schools or teachers.

The next concern, however, was that LEAs might be encouraged to indulge in 'saturation' or 'blanket' testing with a view to making judgements about the effectiveness of institutions. In the 1977 Green Paper, *Education in Schools*,[12] it was suggested that tests suitable for monitoring in LEAs were likely to come out of the work of the APU. LEAs were then urged to wait for this test material but, if they could not wait, to monitor using only a light sample of children.[13] Against this advice, many LEAs introduced their own blanket testing system whereby they tested every child in the target age group rather than the 10 per cent recommended by the DES.

The other big worry was about the APU's effect on the curriculum. Is it possible to have a national system of assessment and not affect the curriculum in some way? In order to develop test items it is necessary to take a model of the curriculum. Will this model then become the dominant model for the curriculum? There was indeed some concern in the early days that the APU was an attempt by the DES to bring in an assessment-led curriculum. The way that it was thought this might come about is essentially an indirect one, by which the APU's curriculum model would provide a framework for local authority assessment and thereby a means for introducing a core curriculum.[14] The pressure on LEAs to monitor their standards has already been discussed, and the danger envisaged lay in the possibility that through 'item banking' procedures and in particular the LEA and Schools Item Bank (LEASIB) project at the NFER it would be possible to link local testing programmes to the APU's national monitoring programme. APU findings would provide a baseline of performance and a core of items from which LEAs would be able to develop their own tests and examine the performance of their pupils. The range of APU items would then provide the common core of a national curriculum. As it happens there are technical problems associated with item banking and it is now apparent that LEAs will not have access to APU-style tests via LEASIB. However, the use by LEAs of actual APU test items is currently being discussed and, while it is still some way off, this link is considered by some observers to be potentially more dangerous, because it is more direct, than the LEASIB link.

THE APU IN 1984

The initial cycle of five annual surveys ended in 1982 for maths, 1983 for language and 1984 for science; the last of the three annual surveys in modern language will take place in 1985. Maths, language and science will then be monitored once every five years; a decision about the future of modern language monitoring has yet to be made. This rolling system of monitoring with maths, language and science taking it in turns will have the function of updating the national picture and identifying trends, while limiting the burden on schools and reducing costs. Each of the teams will produce a retrospective report at the end of their cycle of annual surveys; though the first of these reports is not yet available, it is understood that they will present composite information for the five years and the different ages tested.

The total running costs of the APU in the 1983–84 financial year are expected to be about £1.4m, about £1.2m of which is attributable to monitoring and research.[15] Part of these costs are met by the Education Departments of Wales and Northern Ireland, the remainder (about £1m) being a charge on the DES, and representing about 40 per cent of its research budget. On the basis of the APU's programme as currently planned, DES costs are expected to fall to a little over £500,000 per annum from 1986–87 onwards when all annual monitoring will be completed, but there will be some fluctuations, especially in the years when science is monitored owing to the high cost of practical testing and the three ages involved.

The impact of published reports, particularly on teachers, has been poor and this was a major theme of our 1982 evaluation. In November 1982 the decision was made that more emphasis be put on dissemination. Thus there is a series of occasional papers and there is a regular newsletter; the DES has produced a booklet on the writing performance of 15-year-olds;[16] and the Association for Science Education, acting as the APU's agent, is publishing a series of pamphlets on science performance, aimed at the classroom teacher.[17] The policy on published major reports is that, from the beginning of 1984, these will be produced in limited number by the DES and will be free; reports will no longer be published (at considerable expense) by HMSO. Instead the emphasis is now on short, easy-to-read pamphlets and booklets on specific areas aimed at a specific audience. The APU has also commissioned independent evaluations of maths and language reports. The maths evaluation is based at the Cambridge Institute of Education, the language evaluation is being conducted by an ex-ILEA inspector. (An evaluation of the science work is expected to be commissioned in summer 1984.) It is expected that these independent evaluations will result in pamphlets and documents for in-service training of teachers.

There has been continuing discussion within the Unit, its committees, groups and teams over the nature and extent of the background variables which should be measured. Information of this sort is essential for the interpretation of findings and to provide data of value to policy-makers, that is, to fulfil part of its fourth task—identifying differences of achievement in relation to the circumstances in which children learn. The Statistics Advisory Group has advised against the collection of several proposed variables because of problems of measurement, while the Consultative Committee has been consistently against the collection of home background information from either parents or children. The outcome of a research project based at Leeds, commissioned by the DES to look for a 'surrogate' measure of home background, is awaited. Meanwhile, the current situation is that school-based measures are being collected by the teams in their surveys. However, composite measures of background (both social and educational) have limited potential for explaining performance at an individual or group level. And, as Nuttall[18] has pointed out, there can be little doubt that, in any case, information on classroom processes and detailed curriculum information is vital for interpretation of the survey results. The collection of such data is not compatible with survey techniques but requires more intensive study. In the fallow four-year period between surveys, the teams will have an opportunity to make in-depth studies which were promised when the work was first commissioned. At this point, however, only in-depth analysis of *existing* data is involved; although in-depth studies involving the collection of *new* data are possible, this option has not yet been taken up by the teams.

With regard to making test items available to LEAs and making the data available for secondary analysis by outside researchers, the APU is in favour of both these in principle. However, things are still at the discussion stage. There are problems, of course, about opening the item banks: the DES is concerned not to encourage more blanket testing by LEAs and with some of the test items the marking is extremely sophisticated and training is required. As for the data, the APU accepts that these are a major research resource which should be opened up but with arrangements which safeguard the interests of the monitoring teams.

AN EVALUATION OF THE APU

What then has been the impact of the APU? Have the early fears been realized? How far has the APU fulfilled its tasks?

The first task—to appraise existing instruments and methods of assessment—has varied according to the curriculum area involved. The maths team was always intended to base its work on an assessment of the TAMs material. The language team, on the other hand, following Bullock, would never have used existing tests; as for the science team, there was really nothing available for it to consider using. The discussion documents produced by the Aesthetics and Personal-Social groups, however, include extensive reviews of existing methods of assessment.

It is in dealing with the second task—to sponsor the creation of new instruments and methods of assessment—that the APU can be seen to have had its biggest success. There is no doubt that the teams have produced exciting new material and done pioneering work in the assessment of practical skills in maths and science and in the assessment of oracy. The APU has also broken new ground in sponsoring the assessment of pupils' attitudes as part of the national surveys.

The third task—to promote the conduct of assessment in co-operation with LEAs and teachers—is rather puzzling. If the DES had meant it to mean persuading LEAs to allow the tests to be carried out in their areas and teachers to administer them in the classrooms, then the Unit has certainly succeeded, though the school refusal rate has become worryingly high. If, on the other hand, as seems more probable, this task meant something more active on behalf of the LEAs, for example, LEASIB, then this has not materialized in workable form, though it may with the proposed availability to LEAs of APU items.

On the fourth task, a start has been made on looking at performance in relation to some background measures. However, many of the measures used, for example, pupil/teacher ratio and region of the country, are really of little direct use to policy-makers. More relevant variables which would relate the circumstances in which children learn, for example, size of teaching group, qualifications and experience of the teacher, resources available (particularly for science) and aims of the programme of work, have been used in the later surveys. These are not as relevant as they might appear since, for example, the particular teacher responsible for the class at the time of testing may have been less influential on the children's attainment than other teachers earlier in their education. Moreover, there can be little doubt that this type of information is not best collected via large-scale surveys but in studies of an in-depth type. It is quite clear that any attempt to look at low achievement will have to be via in-depth studies. As for making the findings available to those concerned with resource allocation, as we have said, the findings are of little value to policy-makers and, as they were reported up to mid-1983, of little value to LEAs. However, there is a considerable amount of data which could be 'mined' for its lessons to teachers and this is what the Unit, with its new dissemination policy, is aiming at. Within the Unit the emphasis seems to have shifted away from a concern with information relevant to policy making and resource allocation towards a concern with detailed test information which could throw light on children's cognitive development.

On the Unit's other aims, as outlined in their publicity material rather than in the terms of reference, namely, to provide information on standards and monitor changes in performance over time, there has been little progress. The two are related and no consensus has been reached on how to analyse trends over time. This problem has dogged the APU for several years now (see both Nuttall[19] and Goldstein[20] for an admirably clear discussion of the issue) and is by no means an uniquely British problem. The National Assessment of Educational Progress in the USA has also grappled with it[21] and relies on using a number of items that are common from one survey to the next to indicate change, rather than using the controversial Rasch technique. The problem with this method is that the core of items which is used regularly cannot provide a wholly representative sample of the items used in any particular survey and so the information thus provided on changes in performance over time is inevitably limited. The APU teams are also using some common items from one survey to another, e.g. in maths half the items were common in the first and last annual surveys. At the end of its five-year period of surveying, each team will produce composite measures of performance over the five years which serve as a baseline (or standard) with which to compare performance measured subsequently in the five-yearly surveys. By then, the question of how to analyse trends in performance may have been answered in part. Certainly the Unit, although it said much about standards in the early days, has not attempted to define 'standards' in the sense of acceptable or looked-for performance, and will instead rely on describing measured performance over a period of several years—a far less contentious and more acceptable task—and on comparing relevant changes between groups, e.g. sexes, over time. The DES however is not quite so circumspect: the pamphlet on the writing performance of 15-year-olds was launched as a contribution to the debate on standards 'to trigger a public debate about the content of English teaching and the standards needed' (*TES*, 2 December 1983, p. 3).

What about the early fears? Teachers' concerns that national monitoring, though ostensibly to do with children's performance, could be interpreted as dealing with teachers' competencies have proved to be unfounded. The Unit's adherence to light-sampling techniques, insistence on anonymity and inclusion of teacher union representatives on the Consultative Committee have all helped to allay teachers' fears. The extent to which the APU has carried the teachers with it can be illustrated by some findings of a teacher-interview survey we carried out late in 1982: approximately 70 per cent of the primary and secondary heads interviewed (120) were in favour of national monitoring,[22] with accountability and the need to keep a check on standards to the fore in their comments.

The other concern was about its impact on the curriculum. Would monitoring the four-topic core curriculum result in undue emphasis being placed on these subjects? Would what was tested one year become the curriculum in future years? The answer to the second question is no, because the APU's sampling and testing policies have prevented this happening, and if the answer to the first question is yes, then the impact of the APU on the development of a core curriculum cannot easily be separated from the influence of other factors in education. In 1982, when we published our evaluation of the APU, we felt that any impact there might be on the curriculum would be via the curriculum models adopted by the test development teams; the teams were aware of this and operated on a wide curriculum model so that any impact would be widening not narrowing, and positive not negative. Indeed in 1982 there was a certain ambivalence on the part of the APU towards its role *vis-à-vis* the curriculum. The APU had been accused of being a Trojan horse to bring in an assessment-led curriculum; this, however, was a slightly paranoid view of the role of central government in the educational system without sufficient awareness of the constraints on it through the countervailing power of bodies such as the National Union of Teachers. In order to allay fears, the Unit maintained that it would not attempt to influence the curriculum via back-door methods. That ambivalence about its curriculum role has now gone, and one of the Unit's current major aims is to milk its very detailed survey findings in order to improve curriculum content and delivery—that is, teaching. This is being done via its new policy on reports, the independent evaluations and the commissioned occasional papers referred to earlier. Both APU staff and monitoring teams have given considerable time to inservice courses in LEAs, for which there is great demand particularly in the area of practical testing.

Of course there have been considerable changes in the education scene since 1982 and the APU, with the information it can provide on levels of performance, is particularly relevant to discussions about raising standards set off by Sir Keith Joseph's Sheffield speech.[23] Though there are no formal links between the APU and the two new bodies, the School Curriculum Development Committee (SCDC) and the Secondary Examinations Council (SEC), established by the DES to replace the Schools Council, the APU data will be fed into their committees for their early deliberations. Two particular areas of input are likely to be important in helping to define grade-related criteria and in suggesting modes for the 16+ exams[24]. Of course now the DES has the SCDC, composed of its civic nominees (in contrast to the Schools Council whose members' were nominated by all the partners in the education service), it no longer needs the APU as a means of having some say in the curriculum.

It is instead in the area of providing detailed information to guide teaching practice that the APU's profile now seems to be highest. The incidence of low achievement, changes over time, policy decisions concerning resource allocation, making test items available to LEAs—these are all still on the agenda, but one senses that they are no longer considered to be paramount. These areas are of course potentially far more problematic, particularly given the way the APU carried out its tasks up to 1982. The Unit's achievements, given the scope of the task and the newness of the ground to be covered, should not be undervalued but our view is that given a more careful structuring of early plans and more rigorous forward planning throughout, the Unit could have made more progress than it has. We know that the DES never gave the APU guidance about which policy questions to address. The aim seems to have been simply to develop a national system of assessment that functioned and was acceptable with little thought as to what specific questions it might answer. Indeed it was not until June 1981 that a list was made public, for the first time, of questions the Unit hoped to be able to answer. When the list was analysed, given the way the APU programme turned out, it was possible to provide answers to only a handful of these questions. Why did the Department or the Unit not list more clearly at the outset the policy questions to which they wanted answers? It is possible that the APU was intended solely as a monitoring exercise giving information on overall standards and nothing else. It is possible that the story of the APU is just an example of lack of forward planning. It is also possible that it was a more deliberate policy of leaving all options open in order to gain maximum co-operation from interested professional and lay people. We have concluded that the last two factors both played a part.

In 1982 the APU's future was reviewed within the DES and several crucial decisions were made:

—the dissemination policy was modified so that short, easy to read, cheap publications would be aimed at particular groups in society;

—data would eventually be made available to other researchers for secondary analysis;

—quinquennial monitoring was to be adopted in order to reduce the cost and burden on schools and to allow in-depth analysis of results by the research teams;

—definitive statements about changes in performance over time could not be made for the immediate future.

We believe that these decisions were necessary and for the good. The current moves to disseminate its findings to improve the curriculum—by, it must be admitted, anything but backdoor methods—can be given a cautious welcome (and certainly the demand from LEAs and teachers for courses and conferences seems quite considerable). However, its future impact on the curriculum is uncertain and much will depend on the APU's links with the two new organizations (the SCDC and the SEC) and how these bodies attempt to control the curriculum.

To draw back from musings about the future to comment on the APU at present, we must conclude that, though the APU's work has not to date served policy-makers, it has promoted valuable test developments which serve a broad curricular approach. As a consequence the results of the surveys have a great potential for alerting teachers to areas of weakness in teaching content and method. With the Unit's changing emphasis towards dissemination of interpreted findings this potentially beneficial influence could be released.

NOTES

1. Gipps, C., Steadman, S., Blackstone, T. and Stierer, B. (1983) *Testing Children: standardized testing in local education authorities and schools,* Heinemann Educational Books, London.
2. Gipps, C. and Goldstein, H. (1983) *Monitoring Children: an evaluation of the assessment of performance unit,* Heinemann Educational Books, London.
3. Whenever we use the term 'APU' we are referring to the DES-based secretariat. Committees, groups and teams are always named individually.
4. Report of Sir Keith Joseph's speech to the North of England Education Conference 6 January 1984, in *Education,* 13 January 1984.
5. DES (1976) *The APU—An Introduction,* DES, London.
6. Cox, C.B. and Dyson, A. (1969) *The Fight for Education,* Critical Quarterly Society, London.
7. Report of the Working Group on the Measurement of Educational Attainment (1971) DES, London.
8. DES (1975) *A Language for Life* (The Bullock Report), HMSO, London.
9. Lawton, D. (1980) *Politics of the School Curriculum,* Routledge & Kegan Paul, London.
10. DES (1974) *Educational Disadvantage and the Educational Needs of Immigrants* (Cmnd 5720), HMSO, London.
11. Broadfoot, P.M. (1979) *Assessment, Schools and Society,* Methuen, London.
12. DES (1977) *Education in Schools: A Consultative Document* (Cmnd 6869), HMSO, London.
13. DES (1978) *Assessment in Schools* (Reports on Education No. 93), DES, London.

14. Pring, R. (1980) *APU and the Core Curriculum,* Curriculum and Resource Centre, Exeter University School of Education.
15. Letter from Jean Dawson, Administrative Head of the APU, 19 March 1984.
16. DES (1983) *How Well Can 15-year-olds Write?,* DES, London.
17. See e.g. *APU Science Report for Teachers: 1, Science at Age 11,* Hatfield, Association for Science Education.
18. Nuttall, D.L. (1983) Monitoring in North America, *Westminster Studies in Education,* **6,** 63–90.
19. Nuttall, D. (ed.) (1985) Problems in the measurement of change, in *Assessing Educational Achievement,* Falmer.
20. Goldstein, H. (1983) Measuring changes in educational attainment over time: problems and possibilities, *Journal of Educational Measurement,* **20** (4), 369–377.
21. See note 18.
22. See note 1.
23. See note 4.
24. Personal communication, Arthur Clegg, professional head of APU, 16 February 1984.

Index